W9-BYT-222

The Art of Music Copying

THE PREPARATION OF MUSIC FOR PERFORMANCE

The Art of Music Copying

THE PREPARATION OF MUSIC FOR PERFORMANCE

by Clinton Roemer

ROERICK MUSIC CO.   SHERMAN OAKS, CALIF.

ACKNOWLEDGEMENTS

Grateful acknowledgement is made to the following publishers for permission to quote from their copyrights:

Criterion Music Corporation for A ONE WAY STREET, Words and Music by Van Alexander and Steve Graham

T.B. Harms Company for BLAME IT ON MY YOUTH, Words by Edward Heyman, Music by Oscar Levant

Morella Music Company for ENCHANTED ISLE, Words by Eddie Brandt, Music by Carl Brandt

Wilderness Music Publishing Co., Inc. for THE CHOKIN' KIND, Words and Music by Harlan Howard

Photographs: Joy Thompson
Typography and Production: Your Secretary/Printer

© Clinton H. Roemer 1973

Sole Selling Agent:
Roerick Music Co.
4046 Davana Road
Sherman Oaks, Calif. 91403

PREFACE

Copying music is an art.

Just as it takes more than a brush, paint and canvas to create a painting, so it takes more than a pen, ink and paper to create a written page of music.

A person without any musical knowledge can learn to copy music by rote, without becoming an accomplished copyist. One with a modicum of musical knowledge can, at best, achieve mediocre results. But to become a truly accomplished preparator of music requires a thorough knowledge of the theory of music, harmony, and the ranges, capabilities and limitations of the various instruments. This fund of information must be constantly added to through practice, further studies, observation and experience.

Without training and knowledge, the beginning copyist feels it sufficient to place on manuscript paper all the notes and symbols found in a score in the same manner they were written there:

A qualified copyist would have automatically properly spaced the notes within each measure, and at the same time simplified the part for the player by editing the incorrect notation:

A properly spaced and notated part allows the player to devote full concentration to his performance, rather than being diverted by having to puzzle out a poorly prepared manuscript.

A copyist's true function is to extract the various parts from a musical score, edit and transcribe them in a legible, correct and completely understandable form for the player.

The purpose of this book is to show the techniques and devices employed in properly preparing music for performance in the areas of motion pictures, live and filmed television, phonograph recordings, stage bands, night club acts and publishers of educational music.

The reader should be prepared to spend considerable time in learning to accurately write and place on manuscript paper all the various notes, signs and symbols that make up the written language of music. Much additional effort should be expended in the practice of grouping together all of these various components, in their many permutations, into a well spaced and balanced whole. The correct way of writing each example should become second nature before proceeding to the next example.

Very little information on music copying has appeared in print, and many professional copyists today are self-taught, having learned the craft through years of observation, trial and error; as a result, there are almost as many theories as there are copyists.

Presented here are the writer's own beliefs, developed through thirty years of experience, combined with conclusions drawn from a thorough study of traditional practices. The commercial music business, in general, allows little, if any, time for rehearsal, and the copyist cannot allow any doubt to exist in the player's mind as to what is meant on the written page.

TABLE OF CONTENTS

ACKNOWLEDGEMENTS iv
PREFACE v
CHAPTER   1   GLOSSARY 1
             2   EQUIPMENT, MATERIAL AND SUPPLIES 3
             3   BEGINNING TO WRITE 10
             4   NOTES, FLAGS AND BEAMS 12
             5   RESTS AND MULTIPLE BAR RESTS 23
             6   CLEFS, ACCIDENTALS, SIGNS, SYMBOLS AND ABBREVIATIONS 26
             7   KEY SIGNATURES AND TIME SIGNATURES 44
             8   SLURS AND TIES 48
             9   CHORDS 54
          10   SPACING 61
          11   NOTATION 68
          12   PHRASING 84
          13   EDITING 92
          14   ENGLISH ON PARTS 106
          15   TRANSPOSITION 109
          16   PREPARING A SCORE AND PARTS FOR COPYING 110
          17   COPYING AN ORCHESTRA PART 115
          18   DRUM PARTS 123
          19   GUITAR PARTS 131
          20   PIANO PARTS 139
          21   HARP PARTS 145
          22   STRING PARTS 147
          23   VOCAL PARTS, LEAD SHEETS AND SONG COPIES 155
          24   CHOIR PARTS 161
          25   CONDUCTOR PARTS 166
          26   COPYING FROM SKETCH 177
          27   COPYING FOR PUBLISHERS 180
          28   CLOSING 182
ABOUT THE AUTHOR 183

Chapter 1
GLOSSARY

An explanation of the terms used in this book,
and/or words in common usage among copyists:

ARRANGER .... Represents the person who prepares the score to be copied. For the sake of conformity, mention of composers and orchestrators will be avoided as much as possible.

BAR .... Same as a measure. Bar properly means a bar-line, however, the term has been misused for so long, it has become synonomous with measure. Both words will be used. If a bar-line is meant, it will be so stated.

BLACK AND WHITE PART ..... A part copied on regular manuscript paper.

BRACE .... The symbol ({) used to connect two staves together, indicating that the two staves are to be played simultaneously by the same player. Found most often on harp and piano parts. Also referred to as a "curved bracket" and "moustache".

BRACED PART .... A double line part, such as a piano or harp.

BRACKET .... The symbol ([ ) used on scores to connect individual sections together. In copying, it is sometimes used on choir parts, where it is more proper than the brace.

COL (COLLA) .... Means "with". The direction "col 1st trumpet" located on a different line of the score, indicates that the same notes are to be re-copied.

COME SOPRA .... Means "as before". If the score states, "come sopra 1-8 of letter "B", it indicates to the copyist that this particular section of the score is to be re-written in a new place.

COMPOSITE PART .... All parts in the same section written on one individual part—mainly used for violins.

DACHON PART .... A part copied on onion skin paper in order that two or more parts can be duplicated by a reproduction process. Used mainly for composite parts.

DITTO PART .... Same as a dachon part.

DIVISI PART .... A duet part written on a single stave. Most often prepared for string players, where two musicians sit at the same stand and read from the same part.

DOUBLE LINE PART .... Same as a braced part.

DUPE (DUPED) PART .... Same as a dachon part.

ENGLISH .... Directions written on parts, such as tempo indications, mute and instrument changes, etc.

ENGRAVED MUSIC .... Published music printed from copper plates prepared by an engraver with a set of punch tools and scribes.

HASH MARKS .... The slanted lines (/ / / /) used on guitar and piano parts to indicate rhythm.

LINE .... 1) a musical line (phrase), and 2) a stave—such as, a "single line part" and "ten-line paper".

1

LITERATURE .... Same as "English".

MUSIC PREPARATION .... A term coming into usage as a replacement for "music copying".

ONION SKIN PART .... Same as a dachon part.

PRINTED MUSIC .... Same as engraved music.

SINGLE LINE PART .... A part for one player, as opposed to a divisi part.

SINGLE NOTATION .... Same as a single line part.

SPLIT SCORE .... When two or more copyists are required to work on the same score, it is "split" between them. The score is divided into equal parts, and each copyist works only on his own section. After one copyist finishes a part within his section of the score, he passes it on to the next copyist in line for his continuation. A quick way to turn out work when working on a deadline.

SLASH MARKS .... Same as hash marks.

STAFF .... The five horizontal lines on which music is written

STAVE .... Same as Staff.

STEMS-UP, STEMS-DOWN .... Each line of a duet part has its own set of stems, as opposed to both parts being written with a single set of stems.

SYSTEM .... Two or more staves connected together, i.e., a braced part is a two-system part, a three-line conductor part is a three-system part, etc.

Lines and spaces of the stave will be referred to by number from bottom to top:

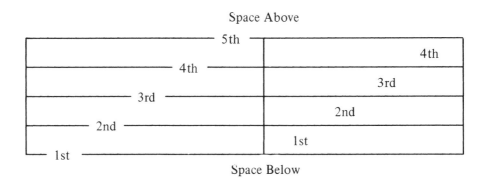

Space Above

Space Below

Chapter 2
EQUIPMENT, MATERIAL AND SUPPLIES

FOUNTAIN PEN AND POINTS .... The most satisfactory point currently available is the *Osmiroid* "Music Writing Point", although it is more flexible than desired. A reasonable substitute is the *Osmiroid* "Italic Medium". The most suitable point, the *Esterbrook* #2312, has been discontinued by the manufacturer. The *Esterbrook* #2314B (also discontinued), could be adapted by removing the nub from the back of the point. The threads on the points of both manufacturers' are the same, and either will fit in the barrel of the other brand. A satisfactory pen point should be like a chisel— able to draw both thick and thin lines, depending upon the stroke used. Most other so-called "Music Writing Pens" on the market are little better than paint brushes, and cannot be recommended.

BLACK INK .... The most readily available is *Monarch Music Writing Ink* manufactured by the Carl Fischer Company in New York City. If not available at a local music store, it can be special ordered. *Higgins Engrossing Ink* is a reasonable substitute. Some specialized music stores carry their own mixture. India type inks are not recommended. They don't flow well and will clog a point within a short time. Ink should be waterproof, for the spray from brass instrument spit valves will play havoc on parts copied with a regular fountain pen ink. The ink used must be opaque— regular ink will not give quality reproductions when used on onion skin paper.

EMERY CLOTH .... One sheet of the finest-grained available. It is used in smoothing out rough areas of pen points.

TOOTH BRUSH........................... The danger of clogged pen points can be minimized by occasionally holding them under a stream of warm water and simultaneously scrubbing them with the brush.

STRAIGHT-EDGES...................... 1) A small 30-60-90 degree triangle, a plastic protractor or a small plastic ruler. Whichever selected, be certain that it has a bevelled edge. This straight-edge will be a constant companion, always held in the free hand in ready availability for ruling beams, bar-lines, stems, first and second endings, etc.
2) A twelve inch plastic ruler (with a bevelled edge) to be used as a guide in printing lyrics on vocal parts, drawing bar-lines on braced and bracketed parts, double bar-lines on scores, etc.

RUBBER CEMENT .... A small bottle with applicator brush.

CORRECTION TAPE .... Single staves (with gummed backing) usually sold in tablet form. Also called "patching tape" or "goof strips". As an alternative, use pieces of regular manuscript paper and apply with rubber cement. (Excess rubber cement, once dried, can be removed by rubbing it with a finger, or with a "ball" made from the dried excess material.)

ELECTRIC ERASER..................... The automatic starting variety with a mercury switch is preferable. Used for erasing mistakes and cleaning ink smudges. Soft white erasers are best. Coarse erasers will either wear a hole in the paper or leave the surface too rough to write on again. Pink erasers will discolor the paper. The electric eraser is also useful in grinding pen points back to a chisel when they have dulled from use—hold the front of the tip at an angle against the rubber as the eraser is running.

3

SINGLE EDGE RAZOR BLADES..Useful in making minor corrections in lieu of an electric eraser. Carefully remove the ink by light scratching. The resulting rough spot should be smoothed with a soft white eraser before writing on the same spot again, otherwise a blur will result.

SPEEDBALL PEN POINT #5
AND HOLDER ....Used in printing song titles on parts

MASKING TAPE .... Preferably the white "flat-back" variety. Used in binding scores and parts. Half-inch width is sufficient, although one roll of inch or inch-and-a-half should be kept on hand for other uses.

SCISSORS .... For cutting correction tape, masking tape and other general uses.

SCOTCH TAPE .... For miscellaneous requirements. It is not recommended for binding scores and parts. The tape doesn't wear well, and eventually becomes brittle and sticky.

SOFT BLACK LEAD PENCILS .... To use in ruling lines onto the stave after the originals were removed while making erasures .

RED PENCILS.............................. For use in marking key and time changes on parts and double bars on scores.

MANUSCRIPT PAPER .... Double sheets of 10-stave paper, printed on one side. It is advisable to keep on hand small quantities of 12-stave paper for special uses, such as for three and four-system parts.

ONION SKIN PAPER .... Again of the 10-stave variety, plus a small quantity of 12-stave for special purposes. Onion skin paper (also called "vellum" or "dachon paper"), is used when more than one copy of a part is needed.

RUBBER-STAMP SETS .... Several different sizes of the *Base-Lock* or *Sta-Tite* brands. The use of stamp sets is a time saver as opposed to hand titling parts with the speedball pen. Following are examples of some of the different sizes and styles of type faces available:

SUNNY

ALWAYS

ALWAYS

SYMPHONY

JOSE FELICIANO

ARRANGED BY

(Most of the material and equipment mentioned is available at most music and/or stationery stores.)

Made to order rubber stamps bearing instrument names are a necessity to the full time copyist. The time saved in stamping parts more than compensates for the cost.

Shown on the following page are imprints from such rubber stamps:

A recommended basic set:

1st	2nd	3rd	4th	5th		DRUMS
	ALTO SAX		TRUMPET	VIOLINS		GUITAR
	TENOR SAX		HORN	VIOLAS		PIANO
	BARITONE SAX		TROMBONE	CELLOS		BASS

If orchestras of more varied instrumentations are frequently encountered, the following are worthwhile additions to the basic set:

CONDUCTOR	FLUTE	ORGAN	VIBES
PRODUCTION	OBOE	ACCORDION	XYLO
VOCAL GROUP	CLARINET	HARPSICHORD	HARP
FLÜGELHORN	BASSOON	CELESTE	TUBA
ENGLISH HORN	SOPRANO SAX	PERCUSSION	BANJO
	PICCOLO	HARMONICA	

The following rubber stamps may be combined with some of those shown above:

GUT STRING	12 STRING	ACOUSTICAL	ELECTRIC
MASTER	RHYTHM	SAX	FENDER
	ALTO	CONTRA	

In order to make combinations such as these:

ALTO FLUTE   BASS SAX   FENDER BASS

GUT STRING GUITAR   ELECTRIC GUITAR

CONTRA BASS CLARINET   RHYTHM GUITAR

CONTRA BASSOON   12 STRING GUITAR

ELECTRIC PIANO   MASTER RHYTHM

Additional rubber stamps that are beneficial:

ON CUE   **TACET**   **SEGUE**

REPEAT TIL FADE

RECOMMENDED BOOKS FOR THE COPYIST

1) A comprehensive book of musical terms.

2) *Orchestration*
   By Cecil Forsyth
   The Macmillan Co.
   New York

3) *Music Notation*
   By Gardner Read
   Allyn and Bacon, Inc.
   Boston, Massachusetts

4) *Range and Transposition Guide to 250 Musical Instruments*
   Compiled and edited by Robert G. Bornstein
   Holly-Pix Music Publishing Co.
   13115 Morrison Street
   Sherman Oaks, California 91403

Shown on the next three pages are the most commonly used manuscript papers. As the size of this book is 8¾" x 12", the examples are slightly reduced from their normal 9½" x 12½" size:

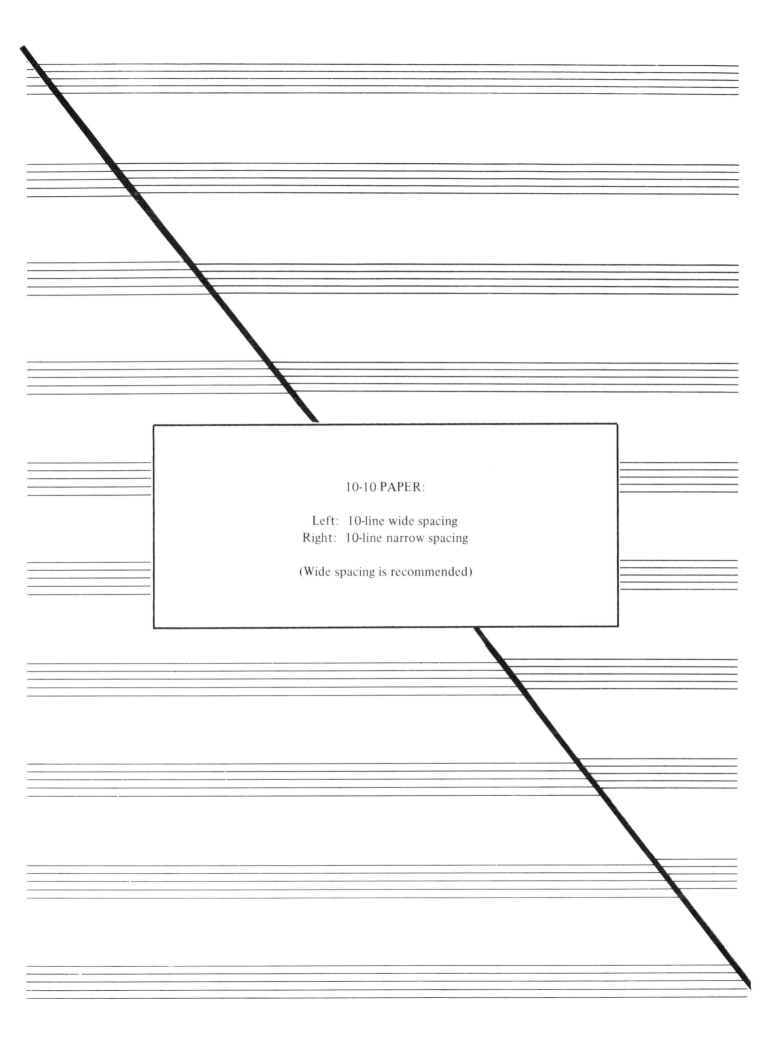

10-10 PAPER:

Left: 10-line wide spacing
Right: 10-line narrow spacing

(Wide spacing is recommended)

12-12 PAPER:

Left: 12-line wide spacing
Right: 12-line narrow spacing

(Wide spacing is recommended)

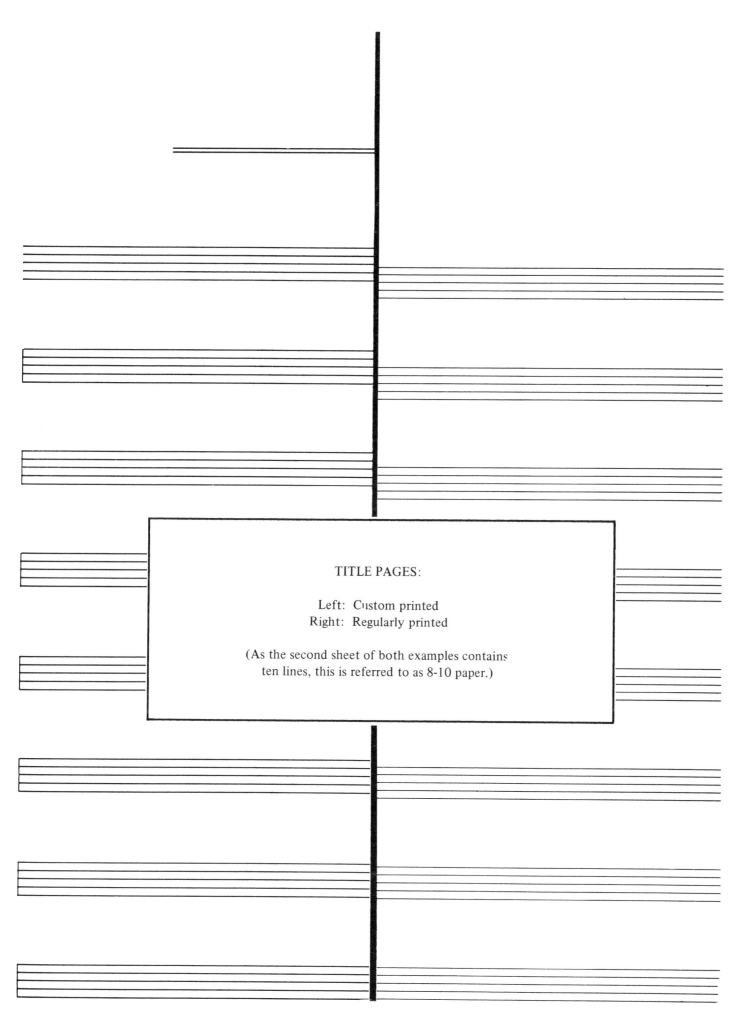

TITLE PAGES:

Left: Custom printed
Right: Regularly printed

(As the second sheet of both examples contains
ten lines, this is referred to as 8-10 paper.)

Chapter 3
BEGINNING TO WRITE

With the amount of "English" to be written on individual parts of music, it is essential to learn to draw easy-to-read numerals and alphabet letters.

Plain block letters, devoid of frills and curlicues, are easiest for the player to read. With little rehearsal time (or even none at all) the player can afford only a passing glance at the written directions on his music; it follows, therefore, that the printing be as legible as possible.

Following is an example of plain block letters and numerals to use as a guide in the development of a personalized and comfortable version. Keep letters "closed", and avoid running them together:

$$ABCDEFGHIJKLMNOPQRSTUVWXYZ$$
$$1234567890$$

A plastic straight-edge is used as a guide for printing by laying it flat on the paper, holding it firmly in place with the free hand and forming the characters by drawing *down* into the top edge. With practice ink smears will be avoided:

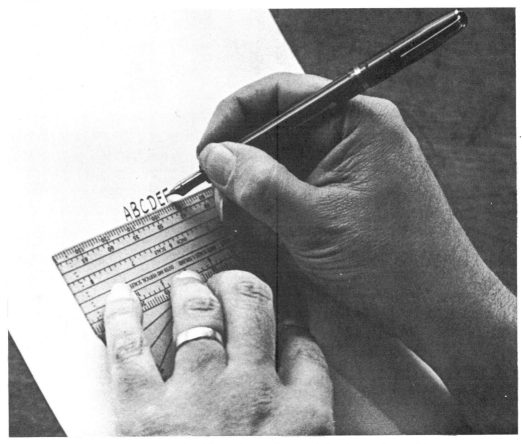

Lower case letters should not be used except for dynamic markings:

$$pp \quad p \quad mp \quad mf \quad f \quad ff \quad fz \quad sfz \quad fp$$

(As a poorly written "p" placed in the vicinity of a lower ledger line note may look like a flat, it is best that a cross bar be drawn at the bottom of the vertical stroke of the "p".)

10

Once the alphabet and numerals have been perfected and a consistency gained in their size and spacing, practice is continued by writing words used in music preparation:

ANDANTE... ALLEGRO... PRESTO... LARGO... RUBATO... A TEMPO

SLOWLY... SLOW 4... FAST-IN 2... IN 3... IN 1... 1ST ALTO

2ND TROMBONE... 3RD TRUMPET... 4TH TENOR... 3RD OBOE

5TH BARITONE... 4TH ENGLISH HORN... DRUMS... GUITAR

PERCUSSION... PIANO... HARP... FENDER BASS... PIZZ... ARCO

CRESCENDO... DIMINUENDO... FASTER... ACCELERANDO... ETC.

The Speedball pen is employed in titling parts. Develop facility in its use by practice in drawing larger numerals and letters:

ABCDEFGHIJKLMNOPQRSTUVWXYZ

1234567890

Once a comfortable technique with the Speedball pen is accomplished, practice is continued by writing song titles. It is important to properly estimate the amount of space needed, concentrating on keeping the title centered on the page:

STARDUST

BEGIN THE BEGUINE

LITTLE GREEN APPLES

WHEN SHE MAKES MUSIC

Chapter 4
NOTES, FLAGS AND BEAMS

For normal handwriting, the pen is usually held at approximately 45 degrees to the horizontal:

In writing music, the pen is held approximately parallel to the horizontal:

Horizontal strokes result in thick lines, while vertical strokes result in thin ones:

Initial practice in writing music manuscript should be confined to the production of hollow note-heads, keeping in mind that *all* notes are slightly egg-shaped. In holding the pen parallel to the horizontal, full advantage will be taken of the thickness of the pen point. Hollow note-heads may be drawn in one of two ways:

1) With two separate connecting strokes:

2) With one continuous stroke:

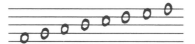

Before beginning practice, examine the following common errors:

1) Round note-heads:

2) Note-heads too large:

3) Note-heads too small:

4) Open note-heads:

5) Overlapped note-heads:

Practice writing a series of ascending and descending whole notes from the space below the staff to the space above. Keep the note-heads squarely on the lines and in the spaces, and strive for consistency in size:

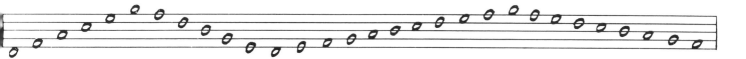

(From the beginning, give full concentration to writing correctly. Good work habits established now will prevent problems later. Poor practices, once adopted, are most difficult to break, and will be potential trouble-makers at rehearsals and performances.)

Practice drawing ledger lines, either free-hand or with the small straight-edge. Ledger lines should be approximately one-fourth of an inch in length, parallel to the lines in the stave, and spaced as nearly proportional to the lines in the stave as the hand and eye allow:

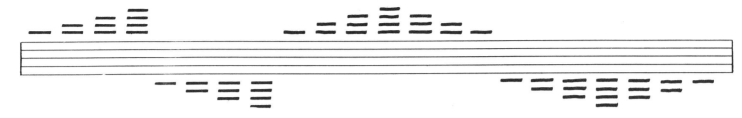

(In actual practice, while working under the pressures of meeting deadlines, few copyists use the straight-edge for other than lettering, beaming groups of notes, and for drawing long lines, such as for crescendos, diminuendos, and first and second endings. Time does not ordinarily permit the use of the straight-edge for ledger lines, stems and bar-lines.)

Continue the practice of drawing whole notes by placing them on, below, and above ledger lines. Notes should be properly centered:

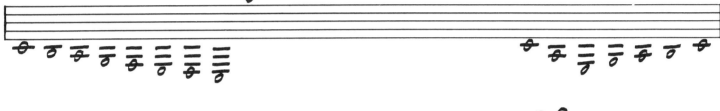

This incorrect example shows ledger lines that are too short for the notes:

In engraved music, the notes in the ledger spaces touch the ledger lines. In manuscript writing, ledger lines are thicker than in engraved music, and the attempt at duplication often leads to overlapped notes.

Consequently these: Are better than these:

Stems and bar-lines are drawn by a vertical stroke of the pen resulting in a thin line. When the stem comes down from the note, it is attached on the left side of the note; when the stem goes up from the note, it is attached to the right side of the note:

Correct: Incorrect:

The proper length of the stem is one octave—exceptions will be noted later in the text:

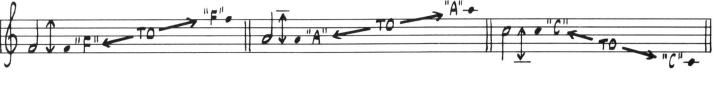

Correct:

Incorrect:

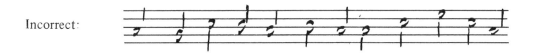

Be certain that stems are always connected to the note-head, and that the notes are not "open":

Incorrect:

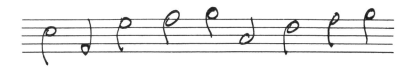

The stroke for a bar-line is always drawn downwards, as is that for a stem—down from the note and down to the note. The note is made as before, while the stem is added as a separate stroke:

PRACTICE: Correctly attach stems to hollow note-heads. Stems may be drawn free-hand, but deft use of the straight-edge for this purpose makes for neater writing. Whichever method is used, it is imperative that the stems be perpendicular to the lines in the stave.

Do not attempt to draw the note and the stem in one continuous stroke without lifting the pen from the paper. This can only result in notes with curved stems which become especially pronounced when done hurriedly:

DIRECTION OF STEMS: The stem is *up* from the note up to and including the second space. From the third line upward, the stem is drawn down from the note:

Stems-Up   Stems-Down

(Some notators state that the stem of the note on the middle line may be drawn in either direction, however, it is recommended that it be drawn only down in the case of single notes. Advantage will be taken of the optional direction in beaming combinations of notes and in stemming chords.)

The location of augmentation dots is governed by the following rules:
1) For notes on spaces, the dot is placed in the center of the same space directly behind the note.
2) For notes on lines, it is placed behind the note and in the space above the note:

Incorrect:

The first exception to the length of stems is in the case of ledger line notes where the stem gradually increases in length with each succeeding ledger line. The stem must always extend into the staff:

Incorrect:

Solid note-heads may be drawn in three different ways:
1) Two separate strokes. A heavier pressure on the point than that used for whole notes will fill in the open space.
2) With three strokes—the two separate strokes as used to draw a whole note, with an added straight stroke to close up the hole.
3) By a swirling continuous stroke. This is difficult to control and its use is not recommended:

Avoid the following common errors:

1) "Open" note-heads:

2) Notes with unconnected stems:

3) Stems on wrong sides of notes:

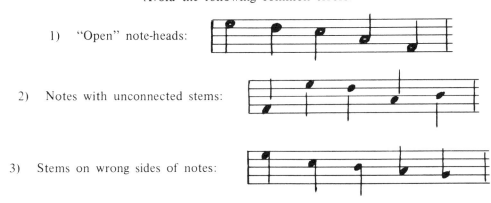

PRACTICE: Draw a series of quarter notes by attaching stems to solid note-heads. Concentrate on keeping stems perpendicular to the lines of the stave, attached to the proper side of the note, and of correct length and direction:

PRACTICE: Go back over previous practice sheets and add augmentation dots in their proper places:

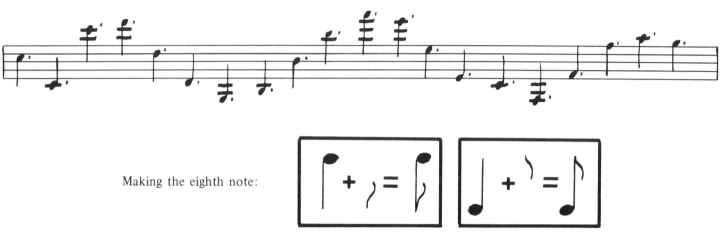

Making the eighth note:

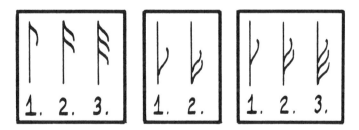

Each segment of a flagged note is made with a separate stroke. The attempt to draw eighth note flags without lifting the point from the paper results in poor work:

To make sixteenth and thirty-second notes:
    1)   Stems up—add each successive flag down from the top.
    2)   Stems down—add stems from the top downward:

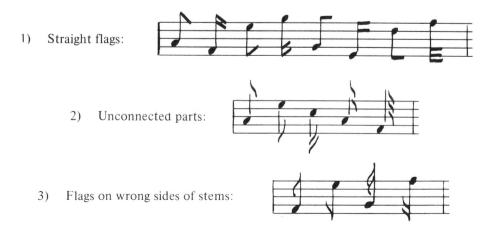

Avoid the following common errors when adding flags to notes:

1)   Straight flags:

2)   Unconnected parts:

3)   Flags on wrong sides of stems:

PRACTICE: Working on the stave from the space below to the space above, attach flags to a series of quarter notes, making them into eighth, sixteenth and thirty-second notes. The length of a stem for an eighth note is the same as for a quarter, but the length must be made progressively longer for each additional flag. Flags are always drawn on the right side of the stem, whether the direction of the stem is up or down:

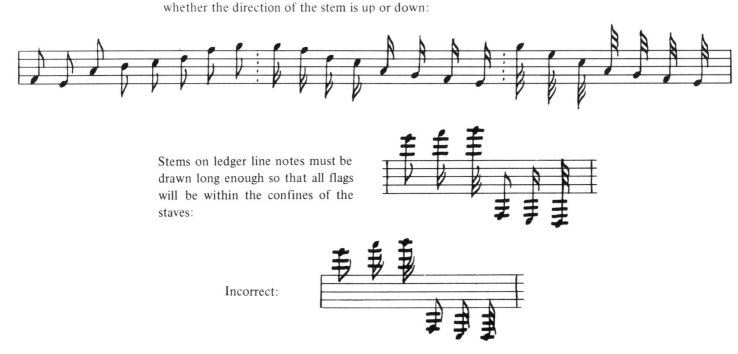

Stems on ledger line notes must be drawn long enough so that all flags will be within the confines of the staves:

Incorrect:

In engraved music, the augmentation dot is placed outside the flag, and the flags are much more florid than those used in manuscript writing where the dot is placed much closer to the note:

Engraved style:    Manuscript:

In duet parts written on the same stave, with each part carrying its own set of stems (stems—up, stems—down), notes are aligned one under the other, except when an interval of the second occurs. In this case the lower note is offset to the right. In the following example, observe how augmentation dots are used when the interval of the second occurs. In the first measure, the notes are dotted according to the rule. In the second measure, an exception occurs—the dot accompanying the lower note must be placed in the space below:

It is incorrect to align stems one under the other:

It is incorrect to offset the top note of an interval of the second to the right:

18

PRACTICE: Draw a series of bar-lines. These must be perpendicular to the lines of the stave, and must cover the complete distance between the top and bottom lines of the stave:

Incomplete bar-lines are inadequate and can cause confusion, as do those that wander at odd angles:

Incorrect:

Beams are used to connect two or more notes together, rather than using a series of separate flags. The first beam is called a "primary beam", and any subsequent ones are called "secondary beams". In order to maintain proper stem length, stems must be made proportionately longer for the addition of each secondary beam:

To beam notes together properly and neatly, it is essential to develop the use of the straight-edge for the purpose. During the practice of lettering, the straight-edge was placed flat on the paper and held firmly in place. For beaming purposes, it is *held* in the hand with only the leading edge touching the paper:

The straight-edge is held above the notes when stems are up:

The straight edge is held below the notes when stems are down:

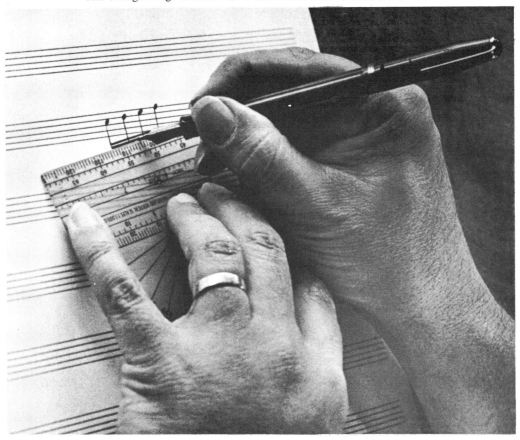

(The type of straight-edge employed—triangular, rectangular, etc.—and the manner of holding it, is a matter of personal choice, and is best determined by trial and experimentation. No hard and fast rule can be made.)

The use of the straight-edge should become an integral part of the copyist's work. Attempting to draw beams free-hand results in slovenly work:

With the occurence of secondary beams, all stems must touch the primary beam:

Correct: Incorrect:

Beams follow the direction of the notes within the group when there is an obvious direction. However, each stem must be of at least the minimum length:

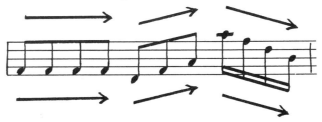

As each stem within a beamed group must be of minimum length, analyze the following example to determine which note(s) dictated the direction of the beam and the length of the other stems within the group:

Beams are never drawn in an arbitrary manner, nor are they drawn in opposition to the direction of the notes within the group. The following are incorrect:

In dotted eighth and sixteenth combinations, the secondary beam always turns inward within its own group:

In beaming ledger line notes, stems must be drawn long enough in order that all beams are inside the staff:

Correct:

Incorrect:

As stated earlier, ledger lines should be proportionate to each other, as well as being as proportionate to the lines in the stave as the eye, hand, and thickness of the pen point will allow. A descending passage must appear to descend, and conversely, and ascending passage must appear to ascend:

Incorrect:

In preceding examples, the stem attached to the note located on the third line has been drawn downward. In beaming, the "optional feature" of drawing this stem in either direction may be used. As a result, certain combinations of beamed notes may be written in two different ways. In the following example, both groups are correct:

In actual practice, the choice of stem direction would be determined by what preceded and/or followed the group:

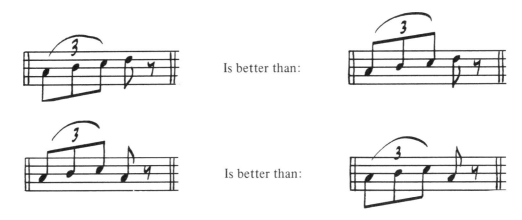

Is better than:

Is better than:

Much time should be spent in the practice of beaming, for the combinations are endless. As an example, any group of three notes has six permutations (1 x 2 x 3 = 6), as:

Any group of four notes as twenty four permutations (1 x 2 x 3 x 4 = 24).

PRACTICE: Beam different combinations of three and four note groups together in all their permutations. Keep in mind that all stems must be of minimum length.

When wide skips occur, as are often found in string parts, the following beaming variant is correct. It may not be used unless all stems are of minimum length:

22

Chapter 5
RESTS AND MULTIPLE BAR RESTS

This chapter is concerned with making rests correctly for manuscript writing. The proper location and spacing of rests within the measure will be covered in Chapter 10.

The whole rest is a thick horizontal line, approximately 3/16 of an inch in length, and is drawn under (and touching) the fourth line of the stave:

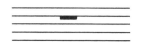

The half rest is a thick horizontal line, approximately 1/8 of an inch in length. It is drawn above (and touching) the third line of the stave:

The quarter rest is drawn from the bottom upward in one continuous motion. It is centered in the stave:

Incorrect variants of the quarter rest.

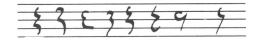

The eighth rest is drawn in one continuous motion, somewhat in the manner of the figure "7". A slight "hook" replaces the horizontal stroke of the "7". The "hook" is placed in the third space:

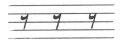

The sixteenth rest is made with three separate strokes. The "hooks" are placed in the second and third spaces, while the connecting stem is drawn slightly longer than that of the eighth rest:

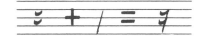

The thirty-second rest is made with four separate strokes. The "hooks" are located in the second, third and fourth spaces. The connecting stem is slightly longer than that used for the sixteenth rest:

The seldom used sixty-fourth and one hundred twenty-eighth rests are further extensions of the eighth rest:

AUGMENTATION DOTS: All dots are placed immediately following the individual rests. Those accompanying whole, half and quarter rests are centered in the third space, while those for eighth, sixteenth and the further extensions, are centered in the space following the top "hook":

Incorrect examples of rests and placement of augmentation dots:

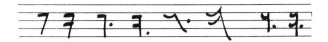

MULTIPLE BAR RESTS – These should be drawn with the aid of the straight-edge. They are placed on the second line and are centered within the measure. The numeral indicating the number of bars of the rest is written above the stave and centered over the heavy bar:

Incorrect Examples:

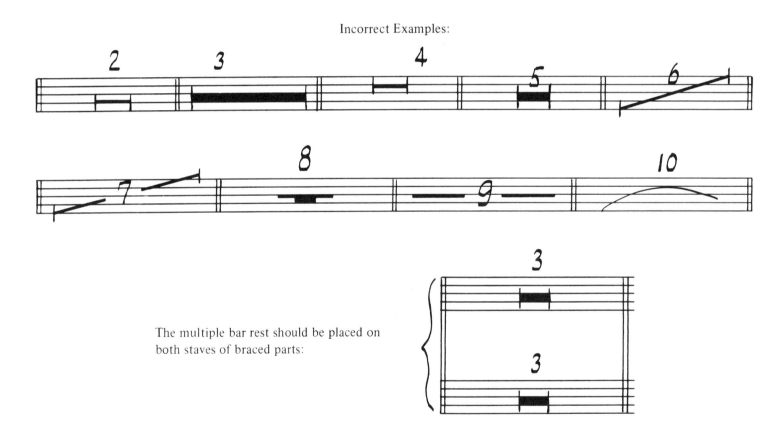

The multiple bar rest should be placed on both staves of braced parts:

Incorrect Examples:

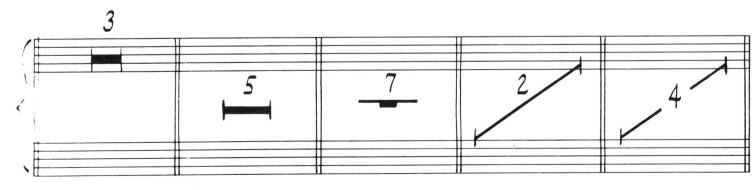

A succession of single bar rests appearing on the score should not be duplicated for the player:

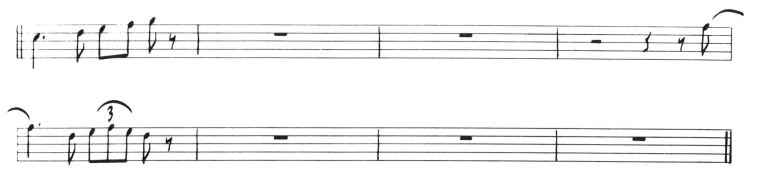

In such cases, make proper use of multiple bar rests:

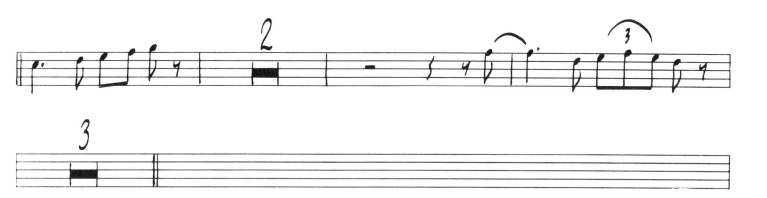

OBSOLETE MULTIPLE BAR REST SYMBOLS:

One should be familiar with the system of un-numbered multiple bar rests once used. The system is un-known to most players today, and consequently, any old parts to be recopied must be converted to the present-day method of rests. In the following example, numbers have been placed below the stave to indicate the number of measures rest indicated by the various symbols. Note that the symbol used today was used only for rests of nine or more measures in duration:

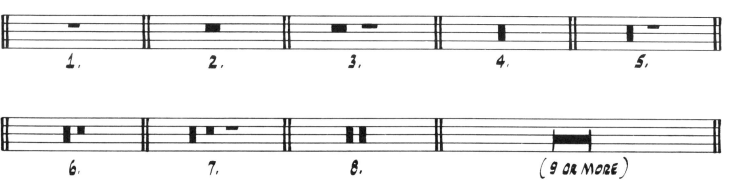

Chapter 6
CLEFS, ACCIDENTALS, SIGNS, SYMBOLS AND ABBREVIATIONS

For all practical purposes, only four clefs need be learned. Middle "C" is shown in the following:

Treble Clef   Bass Clef   Alto Clef   Tenor Clef

(The Treble Clef is best drawn with one continuous stroke from the bottom upward, and the Bass Clef with one continuous stroke moving upward from the third to the fourth space, then downward.)

Examine the clefs used in engraved music for a model. Simplicity is the watchword. There is no need to be florid as in the following:

ACCIDENTALS

The sharp is drawn with four separate strokes: the two downward strokes as thin lines, and the two upward cross strokes as thick lines:

In normal notation, the sharp is not made as a "Tick Tack Toe" symbol, or in an abbreviated manner:

The flat is drawn with one continuous stroke:

It is essential that a flat does not appear as a lower case "b" or as a figure "6". This is especially important in writing chord symbols:

The natural is best drawn with two separate strokes. Note the upward slant to the cross strokes:

Always keep the natural "closed up". Those with rounded corners will sometimes appear to be flats, while those drawn with four separate strokes will frequently result in looking like sharps. Incorrect examples:

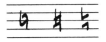

In engraved music, the double sharp is printed somewhat like:

In manuscript writing, a simple "x" is used:

In engraved music, a double flat appears as:

In manuscript writing, a small amount of space is left between the two separate flats:

Incorrect:

The traditional method of cancelling double sharps and flats is now deemed obsolescent:

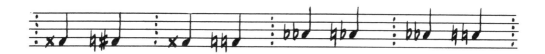

It is correct to state the new accidental without using the superfluous naturals:

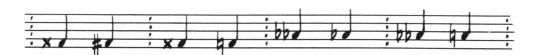

Accidentals are placed squarely on the line or space directly in front of the note they affect:

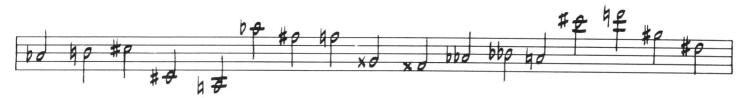

Do not allow them to wander out of position or become too large:

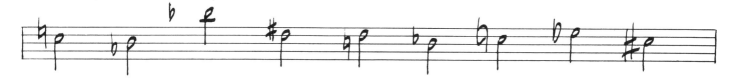

Above all, accidentals must not touch the notes, or another accidental. They must always be drawn in a manner that is crystal clear to the player. Nothing like the following should ever be written by the copyist:

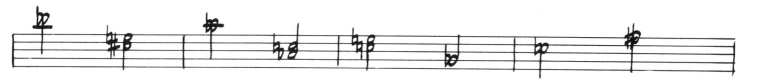

To avoid an overabundance of accidentals, passages such as the following:

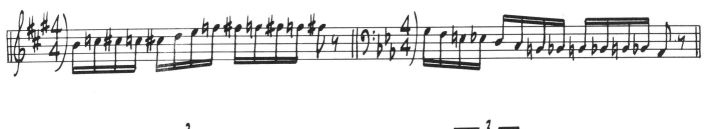

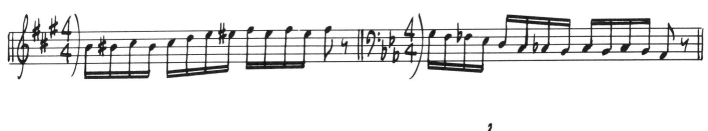

are better written as:

(Never use B-sharps, E-sharps, C-flats, F-flats, double sharps and flats in an indiscriminate or arbitrary manner.)

PAUSE MARKINGS

1) Luftpause ("Railroad Tracks"): Used to indicate a short pause. The symbol is made with two parallel slanted lines and is placed at the top of the stave:

2) Breath Mark: A comma placed slightly above the top line of the stave and between the two notes where the breath is to be taken:

3) General Pause (Grand Pause): The abbreviations "G.P." is placed above the stave over a rest:

Proper uses of the fermata:

1) In the case of notes within or below the stave — placed slightly above the top line of the stave and directly over the note affected.

2) In the case of ledger line notes above the stave — directly over the note.

3) Rests — placed in the space above the stave and centered over the rest.

4) Braced parts in which all notes are sustained — one fermata per stave, each being placed directly over the top note of the chord and in the space above the stave. In the case of upper ledger line notes, the fermata is placed directly over the note.

5) Braced parts with moving voices — the only occasion where the fermata is written upside down. In this case they are placed under the bottom line of the stave, or under the note if a lower ledger note is involved.

6) Traditionally, a fermata is not placed over a luftpause or a general pause. However, for the sake of clarity, its use is recommended in contemporary writing.

Fermati are never placed within the confines of the staff:

Fermati should be drawn boldly, not in a timid manner:

(A fermata is sometimes called a "bird's eye".)

In music prepared for night club acts, the word "dialogue" is frequently used as an alternative for "G.P.' It may be written on the part in one of the two following ways, with the second being preferable:

When a "dialogue" is written on the score as:

For the sake of clarity, it is better to add an extra measure, and write it as follows:

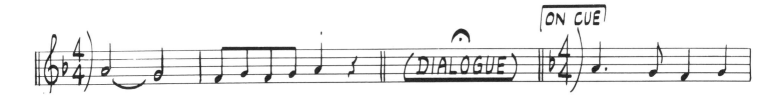

(It is recommended to reiterate the key and time signatures following the use of a "dialogue".)

CRESCENDO AND DIMINUENDO MARKINGS

Wedges ("Hairpins") —   These markings indicate the crescendo and diminuendo. Short wedges may be drawn either free-hand or ruled with the straight-edge, the latter being preferable:

It is imperative that long wedges be drawn only with the straight-edge:

When the full length of wedges is given on the score, copy them correctly:

Do not abbreviate them as in the following:

(Always keep the player informed as to the intent of the arranger.)

On occasion, the score will indicate a crescendo and/or diminuendo with the word(s) rather than wedges. In this case, the abbreviations "cresc" and "dimin" should be used. These directions are written below the stave along with a dashed line showing the length of the passage affected:

The dashed line is also used for a crescendo or diminuendo poco a poco:

A poco a poco crescendo or diminuendo may also be written as:

The dashed line is also used for:
1) Rit. poco a poco
2) Accell. poco a poco
3) Rit. e dimin. poco a poco
4) Cresc. e accel. poco a poco

(In all cases, the word "diminuendo" is preferable to "decrescendo".)

THE GLISSANDO

A glissando is indicated by a wavy line leading from one note to another:

The indication should not be abbreviated:

When a glissando leads from the last note in the last measure of a line to the first note of the first measure of the next line, the player should be given an indication of where the glissando is leading:

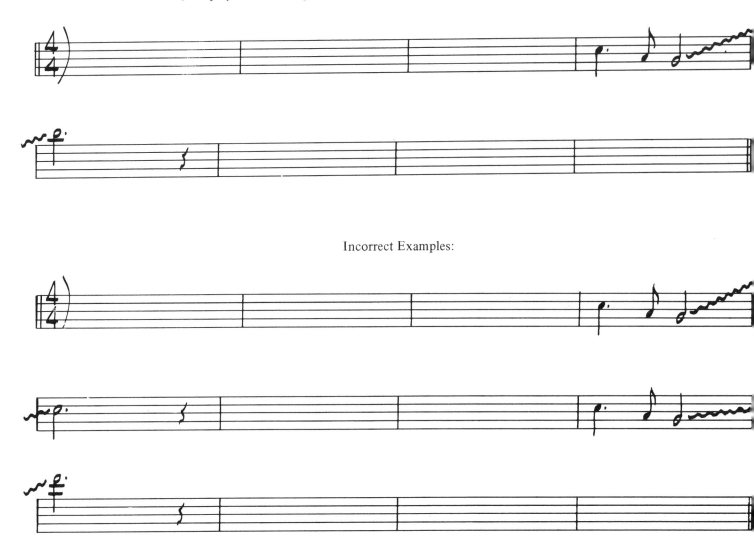

Incorrect Examples:

Although the wavy line is sufficient indication of intent, some arrangers add the word "gliss" as well. Even though this practice is redundant, it does add clarification:

(Either upper or lower case letters may be used. This is one of the few exceptions for the use of lower case printing.)

GRACE NOTES

All component parts of grace notes, including accompanying accidentals, are made smaller than normal size notes, and are placed closely in front of the note they lead to. A single grace note is written as a small eighth note with the addition of a slanted line drawn through both the stem and the flag. Two or more grace notes are written as small sixteenths, but without the addition of the slanted line.

In traditional practices, grace notes are written with or without a slur leading from under the grace note to the principal note. In manuscript writing, it is advisable to use the slur. Again, traditionally, stems are written either up or down. In manuscript practices, more clarity exists by writing all stems up, regardless of whether the notes appear in the staff or on ledger lines. Thirty-second grace notes are sometimes used in traditional music for extremely slow tempos. For practical purposes, properly written sixteenths show the intent just as well:

Incorrect Examples:

An exception to stem direction of grace notes must be made for the lower voice of a divisi part, where the stems must be written down. Be certain that the principal notes are aligned one under the other. A principal note is not aligned under or over the grace note of the other part:

Correct: Incorrect:

Although grace note accidentals do not affect like notes within the same measure, it is preferable that they be cancelled:

Correct: Preferable:

DYNAMICS

Dynamic markings are placed only beneath the stave, slightly before the note or passage affected:

It is incorrect to offset dynamics or to place them directly under a note:

A "p" should never be made that appears to be a flat:

Incorrect: 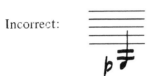   Correct: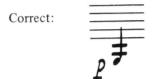

An exception to the placement of dynamics exist in the following instances, where they are written directly under the notes. Such markings are always written beneath the stave:

It is incorrect to place these markings within the confines of the stave, or to offset them:

REPEAT SIGNS

Repeat signs should be made boldly enough to catch the player's eye:

(Note that "back to back" repeats are drawn separately.)

The following are not only incorrect, but would give a player difficulty in attempting to locate them:

Repeat signs on braced
parts should also be
made in a bold manner:

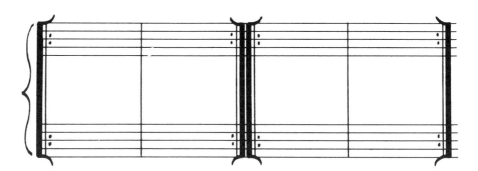

The following variants are incorrect:

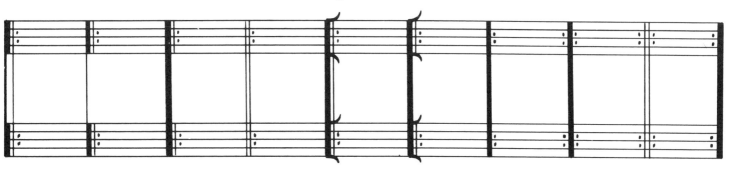

The lines encompassing first and second endings should be drawn with the aid of the straight-edge rather
than free hand:

(It is recommended to use a double bar at the beginning of the
first ending—it serves the purpose of an "eye-catcher" for the
player.)

The following variants are seen in manuscript writing—their use is not recommended:

A first ending continuing from one line to the next, is drawn as:

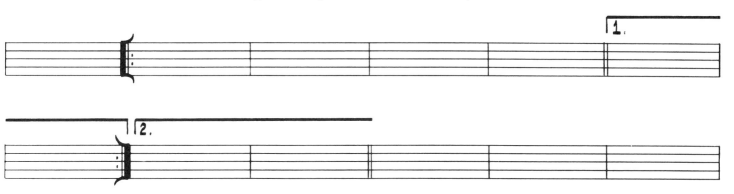

(Poor phrasing, such as in the above example, can be
avoided. Proper phrasing will be discussed in Chapter 12.)

If a repeated phrase is to be played one time and tacet the other, the direction is either:
1) "PLAY 1X ONLY" (or "1X ONLY")–preferable to the direction "TACET 2X"
2) "PLAY 2X ONLY" (or "2X ONLY")–preferable to the direction "TACET 1X"
(Through usage, "X" is the acceptable abbreviation for "TIME", and "X'S" for "TIMES".)

If a repeated section is to be played more than the normal twice, the exact number of times the passage is to be played should be clearly marked, and the number of endings adjusted accordingly:

(As the direction "REPEAT 3 TIMES" can cause confusion, it should not be used. A passage played twice is only repeated once, while one played three times is repeated twice. An arranger who states "REPEAT 3 TIMES" on his score probably doesn't mean it. Check to see his true intent and give the player the proper direction.)

In the following "3 X'S" example, the player is informed to play the first and third times, and remain tacet the second. It is not necessary to add "TACET 2X", for this is obvious from the existing direction:

Other directions that might occur in a repeat section·marked "PLAY 3X'S" are: "PLAY 1X ONLY", "PLAY 2X ONLY". "PLAY 3X ONLY", "PLAY 1X & 2X, and "PLAY 2X & 3X".

(The type of "box" being used to enclose the "English" placed above the stave is recommended for all such directions, as it acts as an "eye-catcher" for the player. It is advisable to omit the bottom line of the "box", for a fully "boxed" direction can often appear to belong to the stave above.)

A final double bar is used at the end of each part:

It is not made as a plain double bar:

It is not necessary to be florid, or to add the word "FINE":

Dal Segno and Coda signs are placed above a double bar, and are best fully "boxed", either in ink or with a red pencil. The latter is preferred as it is a further aid to the player in being able to locate the signs quickly:

ACCENT MARKINGS

The most common accent marks are the following:

- (•) Staccato—very short.
- (ʌ) Short and percussive. It is not written (v) unless under a note.
- (>) Less percussive but longer in value than (ʌ). Not written as (<).
- (−) Note is held full value.
- (≥) Marcato + full value. Not written as (≶) unless under a note.

In traditional practices accents are located:

1) Stems down − over the note and outside the limits of the stave.
2) Stems up − under the note and outside the limits of the stave.
3) Staccato markings are sometimes located within the stave, but are only placed in a space:

Accent marks that leap around (as in traditional writing), also cause the player's eyes to leap around. Therefore, it is preferable to keep all accents above the notes, and outside the stave, regardless of stem direction:

In general, accents follow the direction of the notes:

Correct: Incorrect:

(Additional information on placement of accents, along with exceptions, will be discussed in Chapter 8.)

REPEAT MEASURES

Single bar repeats are made with a thick slanted line between the second and fourth lines of the stave, with the addition of dots in the second and third spaces. The symbol is centered in the measure between the two bar lines:

(With the occurrence of successive one bar repeats, the measures should be counted for the player by the addition of numerals placed above the stave and centered over the abbreviation.)

Repeat symbols are abbreviations and must not be abbreviated further. In the following example, would the player interpret the abbreviations as being repeat bars or as poorly made whole rests?

Two bar repeats are made with two thick slanted lines between the second and fourth lines, bisecting a bar-line, and with the addition of two dots—one to the left of the bar-line in the third space, the other to the right of the bar-line in the second space. The figure "2" is always included, being centered over the bar-line in the space above the stave:

(The length of slanted lines that has been given for one and two bar repeats, is as it occurs in engraved music. In manuscript practices, the lines are generally somewhat longer, but are still centered within the stave.)

The following variants of two bar repeats are incorrect:

38

One and two bar repeat signs should be
written on both staves of braced parts:

The following variants are incorrect:

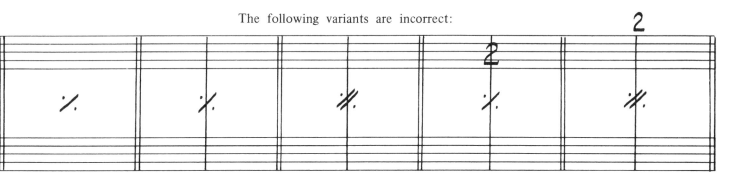

Although three and four bar repeats are used on scores, they should never be given to the player. Repeats
such as the following should be copied out in full:

SINGLE NOTE REPEATS

The abbreviation for a single note repeat is a thick slanted line placed between the second and fourth lines
of the stave. This abbreviation is most commonly used on rhythm section parts (drums, guitar, bass and
piano), and for ad lib solos on instrumental parts:

Single note repeats should be used only as in the above example—never as in the following:

The preceding example written correctly:

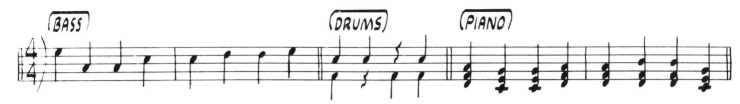

TREMOLANDOS, TREMOLOS AND TRILLS

Tremolandos are indicated with three thick slanted parallel lines. In the case of whole note tremolandos, the three lines are centered between the two notes, and their direction (up or down), is determined by the direction of the interval. In the case of beamed tremolandos, the beam acts as one of the slanted lines, so only two are added. Their direction follows that of the beam:

The following are incorrect:

(In manuscript practices, the thirty-second tremolando is the only one used. In traditional practices, a sixty-fourth is used in slow tempos, and a sixteenth in fast ones. Also, traditionally, the slur is not always used, whereas in manuscript writing it is.)

Tremolos are used in writing for string instruments, mandolin, drums, xylophone, marimba, etc. Tremolos must have exactly three strophes through the stem – each beam acts as a strophe:

(Keep in mind that when writing tremolandos and tremolos, that stems must be made slightly longer than normal in order to accommodate the symbol.)

The following tremolos are incorrectly written:

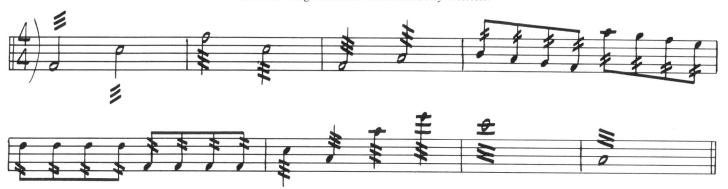

In a so-called "honky-tonk" piano part, a tremolando melody in the right hand may be written as a tremolo:

In opposition, when tremolandos occur as a bass figure in the left hand, they are written as tremolandos, and not as tremolos:

Remember that a tremolo requires three strophes, with a beam acting as one of them. An incorrect example such as the following:

Would be interpreted by the player as abbreviations for sixteenth notes, and would be played as:

The most common ways of writing trills:

Observe that:

1) The wavy line is not used for notes of short value.
2) With notes of longer value, the wavy line runs for the full length of the note.
3) There are three different ways of writing "trill flat" and/or "trill sharp".
4) The terminal group leading from a trill is not always written. When it occurs, the notes included are written as grace notes.
5) Another exception to the use of lower case letters exists–"tr" is used instead of "TR".

The following are incorrect uses of the trill symbol:

OTTAVA ALTO & BASSA

Although it is usually best to write a passage exactly where it sounds, on occasion it becomes necessary to use the "8VA" indication. This direction should be "boxed" and a broken line extended over the full length of the passage affected. The direction should be repeated if the passage is broken up with rests. The direction "LOCO" (as is) is used to return the player to where the notes actually sound:

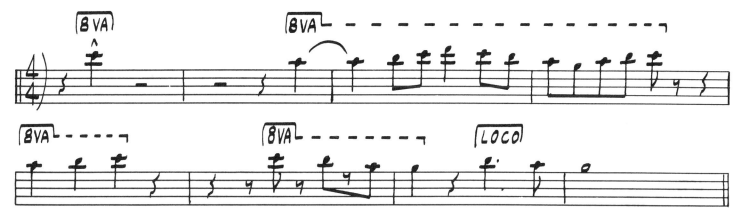

(The direction "8VA BASSA" — meaning, played one octave lower — should not be used other than for passages in the left hand of piano and organ parts, and then only when absolutely necessary. The direction is written out in full, and is not abbreviated as "8 VB".)

JAZZ NOTATIONS

Following are some of the more commonly used jazz notations and the proper way of writing them. There is no standardization for these notations. Their names and interpretations differ from person to person and from one locality to another. Some of the indications should be "boxed". Do not abbreviate "GROWL" as "GR", nor "FLUTTER" as "FL" or "FLTR":

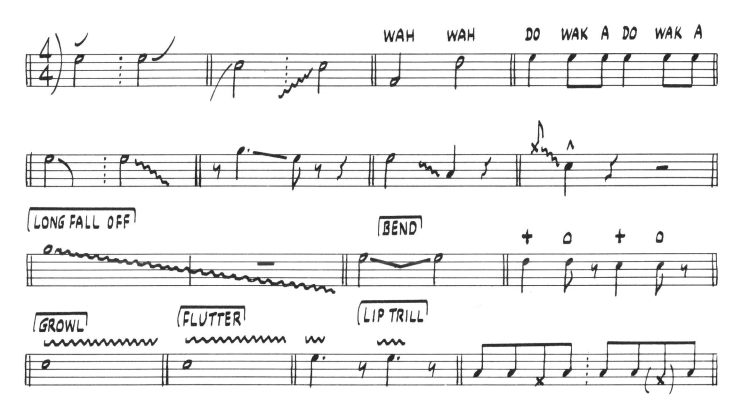

43

Chapter 7
KEY SIGNATURES AND TIME SIGNATURES

The following chart shows the proper placement and location of sharps and flats in all key signatures in the four most commonly used clefs:

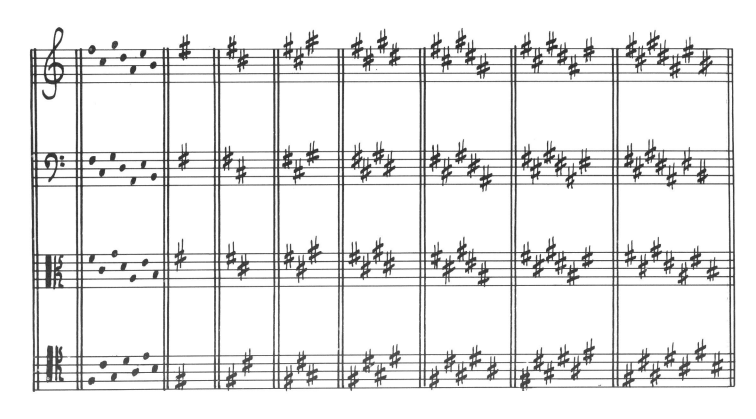

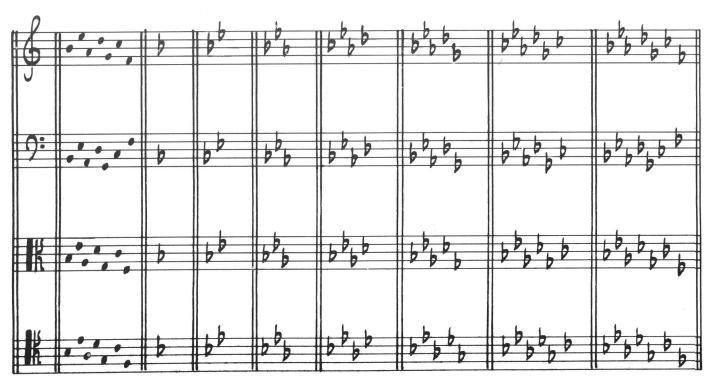

The initial key signature is placed following the clef, and in turn is followed by the time signature. When a subsequent change of key and time occurs, the key is written first and is followed by the time signature. The repetition of the clef is not necessary:

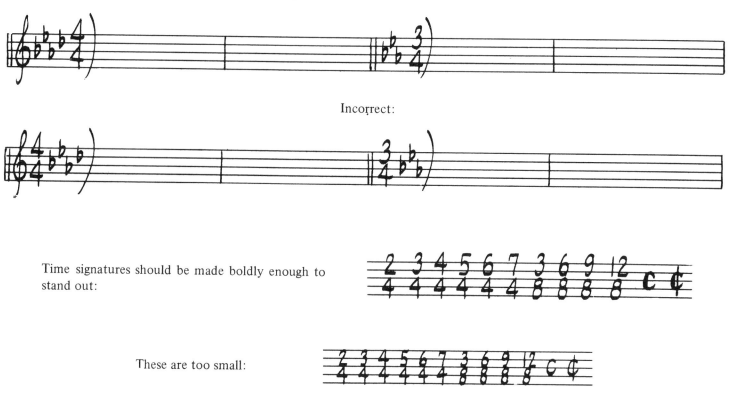

Incorrect:

Time signatures should be made boldly enough to stand out:

These are too small:

To indicate a key change within a composition, it is sufficient to merely state the new key. The traditional method of cancelling out the accidentals of the previous key is obsolescent, and not necessary except when the change is to the key of "C". As an "eye-catcher", it is recommended that an "arc" be drawn on the right side of the signature with a red pencil:

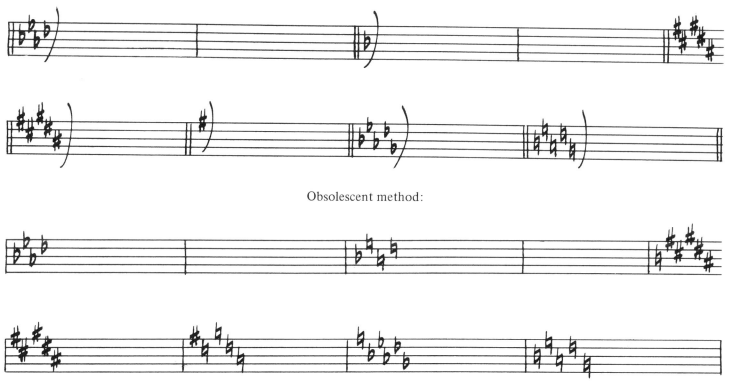

Obsolescent method:

When a key change, time change, or both, is to occur at the beginning of a line, it is best to forewarn the player by pre-stating the change at the end of the preceding line:

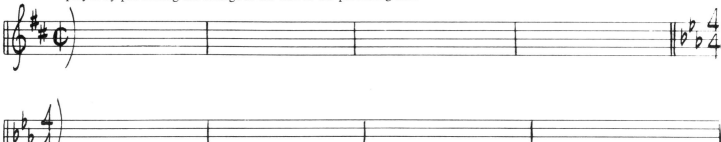

When a key change occurs in the middle of a line, it is advisable to repeat it at the beginning of the next line. A red "arc" is used at the change, and a black one at the "reminder" at the beginning of the line.

(A "reminder" of the key, also with a black "arc", should also be given at the beginning of each new page.)

Any change occurring at a repeat sign is indicated outside of the sign. A repeat sign is not properly considered to be a bar-line, so the previous measure must be completed with a bar-line before the change is made:

Incorrect:

(Traditionally, the clef and key signature are carried; that is, each is written at the beginning of each line of the page. This is also an obsolescent practice, and is seldom done today other than at the request of the arranger, or as a safety factor.)

The traditional method of indicating time changes:

PRACTICE: Recopy the above example. Draw a double bar and a red "arc" at each time change, then observe the additional clarity that has been attained. While such niceties are more laborious, the time is well-spent and the results gratifying.

Chapter 8
SLURS AND TIES

Slurs between only a few notes, or very short phrases, are drawn:
1) Under the note-heads when the stems are up.
2) Above the note-heads when the stems are down.

Incorrect use of short slurs:

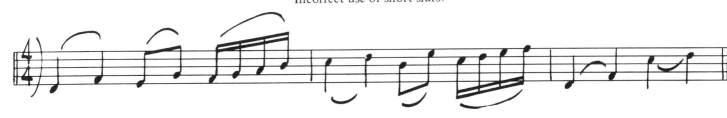

In short groups, where the stem direction is mixed, the slur is drawn above if one or more of the stems is down:

Incorrect:

Correct examples of short slurs:

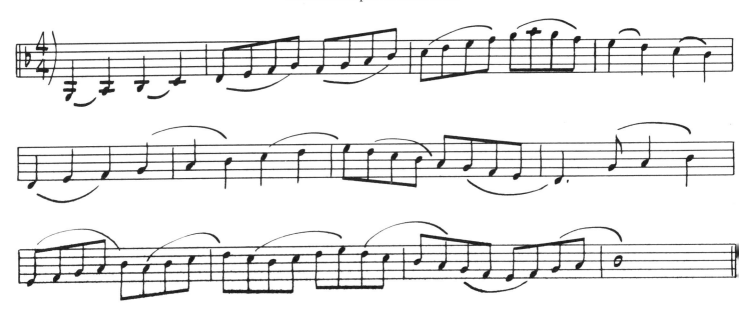

The same example showing incorrect use of short slurs:

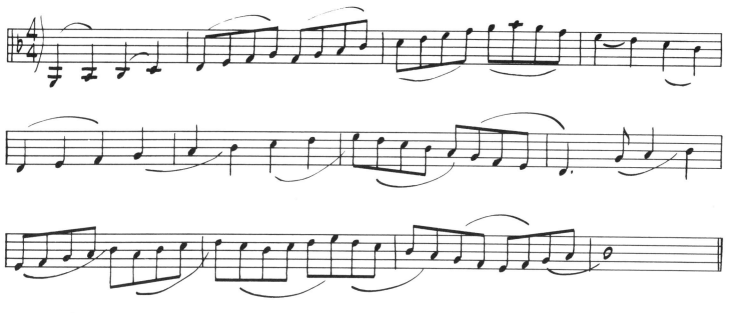

In traditional writing, staccato marks are placed between the note and the slur, regardless of whether the stems are up or down:

In traditional writing, it is incorrect to place staccato marks outside the slur:

In traditional writing, accent marks (other than the staccato) are placed outside the slur:

In traditional writing, it is incorrect to place accents (other than the staccato) between the slur and notes·

The traditional method of writing accents cannot be recommended for manuscript writing. In the following example, written according to traditional rules, observe how the player's eyes would be forced to jump in reading the part:

It is recommended (and preferred by players), that *all* accents be placed above the notes and outside of the slurs:

Long phrases are slurred above the notes regardless of stem direction:

Incorrect:

An exception occurs in divisi writing—slurs (either long or short) are written above the top notes and under the lower notes:

Long slurs are drawn with one continuous arc:

It is incorrect to fragment a long slur:

Ties are drawn:

1) Under the note-heads when stems are up, or in the case of whole notes occurring anywhere lower than the second space.

2) Over the note-heads when stems are down, or in the case of whole notes occurring on the third line and higher.

3) As close to each note-head as the hand and eye allow.

Incorrect uses of the tie:

An exception to the direction of the tie is made in divisi writing. The tie is always "up" on the top part, and always "down" on the lower part:

Incomplete ties may be seen on scores. Quite naturally, these must not be used by the copyist:

When ties occur at the beginning and/or end of a phrase, an accompanying slur must cover the entire phrase:

It is incorrect to draw such slurs in an incomplete manner:

As already stated, the slur is drawn beneath the notes in short phrases with stems up:

However, if ties are present on such short phrases, the slur is drawn above the notes:

In the following incorrect example, the slur is either on the wrong side of the notes, or does not cover the complete phrase:

Correct use of ties connecting notes of different stem directions:

Incorrect use of ties connecting notes of different stem directions:

Unnecessary ties should not be used:

The above example notated correctly:

The use of ties and slurs connecting two notes are the same in divisi writing regardless of whether one or two sets of stems are used:

In divisi writing where long slurs are involved, two separate slurs are required in stems—up, stems—down writing, whereas only one slur is needed if both notes are on the same stem:

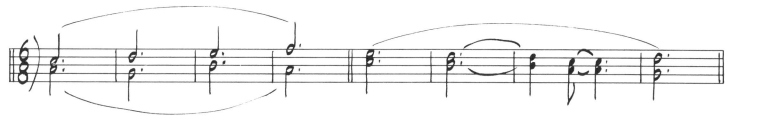

Note in the following example that tremulants are always slurred. Observe the correct use of ties:

(The use of slurs and ties in chordal writing will be discussed in the next chapter.)

Chapter 9

CHORDS

If all notes in a chord are of the same value, they are connected with a single stem. The proper length of the stem is determined by:

1) Stems up–from the top note of the chord.
2) Stems down–from the bottom note of the chord.

<table>
<tr><td>The direction of the stem is up when there are more notes (or wider intervals) below the third line than there are above:</td><td></td></tr>
</table>

<table>
<tr><td>The direction of the stem is down when there are more notes (or wider intervals) above the third line than there are below:</td><td></td></tr>
</table>

In chordal writing, advantage may be taken of the optional stem direction feature of the note on the third line. This will result in being able to write certain chords in one of two ways:

(The major consideration in determining stem direction of chords such as those in the preceding example, would be to attain a consistency with the chords that precede and/ or follow the one in question.)

Although stem directions in the following example are correct:

The choices made in the next example are preferable as a consistency has been achieved:

54

Dyads consisting of an interval of the second are written:

1) Stems up—the top note is offset to the right of the stem. The same configuration is used for whole notes

2) Stems down—the bottom note is offset to the left of the stem. Again, the same configuration is used for whole notes:

Incorrect:

In manuscript writing, full chords containing an interval of the second in the top two voices, or the bottom two voices, are written as follows:

1) Occurring in the top two voices of a chord with stems up—the lower of the two notes is offset to the right.

2) Occurring in the bottom two voices of a chord with stems up—the next to the lowest note is offset to the right.

3) Occurring in the bottom two voices of a chord with stems down—the next to the lowest note is offset to the left:

In traditional practices, the interval is handled in a different manner:

1) Occurring in the top two voices of a chord with stems up—the upper note is offset to the right.

2) Occurring in the bottom two voices of a chord with stems up—the lowest note is offset to the right.

3) Occurring in the bottom two voices of a chord with stems down—the lowest note is offset to the left:

(Manuscript practices are recommended in all the above cases, with the approval of most harpists, guitarists and pianists.)

An interval of the second occurring in the top two voices of a chord with stems down is written in manuscript the same as traditionally—the lower of the two notes is offset to the left:

Incorrect:

55

PRACTICE: Copy the following chords and continue by writing similiar ones:

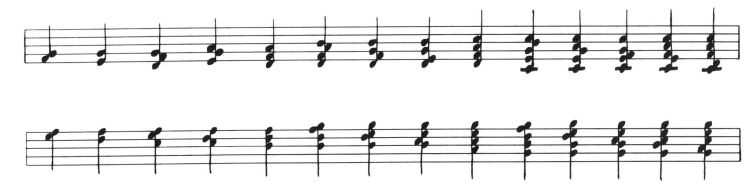

Analyze the following example to determine how the direction of the stems was decided:

Frequently encountered in harp and piano parts is a situation where both hands are written on the same stave. Observe that when an interval of the second occurs between the two parts, that it is not possible to align all the notes of the lower chord under the top one. In such cases, the left hand part must be offset slightly to the right:

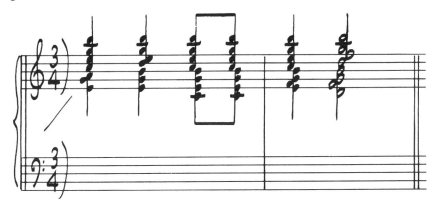

In connecting dyads, the top tie is always up and the bottom tie is always down:

(In any chord written on one stem, the top tie is always up and the bottom tie always down.)

In connecting three note chords (not containing an interval of the second), the direction of the inner tie is determined by the third line of the stave:

    1)   For notes on the third line, the tie may go either direction, but preferably up.

    2)   For notes below the middle line, the tie must be down.

    3)   For notes above the middle line, the tie must be up:

In connecting four note chords (not containing an interval of the second):

    1)   The top two ties are always up.

    2)   The bottom two ties are always down:

In connecting five note chords (not containing an interval of the second), the top two ties are up and the bottom two ties are down. The direction of the middle tie is again determined by the third line of the stave:

    1)   For notes on the third line, the tie may go in either direction, but preferably up.

    2)   For notes below the middle line, the tie must be down.

    3)   For notes above the middle line, the tie must be up.

When an interval of the second occurs in either the top or bottom two voices of a chord, previously given rules cannot apply, as will be obvious in the following incorrect example:

PRACTICE: Copy the following example, and observe the exceptions that must be made in tieing because of the occurrences of the second:

A further exception exists in the case of piano and harp music when both hands are written in the same stave. In this case, *all* ties in the right hand part are up, while *all* those in the left hand part are down:

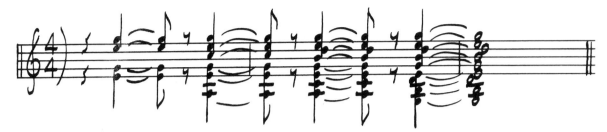

When two chords are slurred together, only one slur mark is necessary:

As the intent is clear with the one slur, it is not necessary to place slur markings between all notes in the two chords:

(Do not confuse this rule with that for divisi writing, where both notes must be slurred.)

For long phrases, one slur above the notes is correct:

In chordal writing, exceptions must be made to the rule governing stem directions when a moving voice, or voices, occur:

The following are incorrect:

(Study engraved piano music for further examples.)

RULES GOVERNING THE LOCATION OF ACCIDENTALS BEFORE CHORD MEMBERS

1) Two accidentals in a chord where the interval between them is a sixth or less:

2) Two accidentals in a chord where the interval between them is a seventh or more:

(In engraved music, this rule begins to apply when the interval between the accidentals is a sixth. However, this is difficult to accomplish in manuscript writing because of the danger of running the two accidentals together.)

3) Three accidentals in a chord where the interval between the two outside accidentals is a sixth or less:

4) Three accidentals in a chord where the interval between the two outside accidentals is a seventh or more:

5) Four accidentals in a chord. (As the outside interval is usually at least a seventh, the lowest accidental is aligned under the uppermost one):

(Exceptions to the rule always exist, and at times it may become necessary to improvise, such as when the outside interval is a sixth or less):

59

6) Five accidentals in a chord:

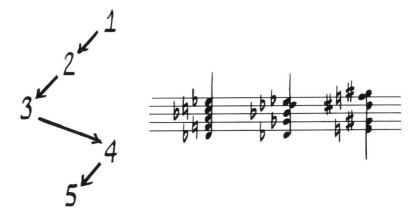

7) Six accidentals in a chord, such as may occur in piano and harp parts when both hands are written on the same stave:

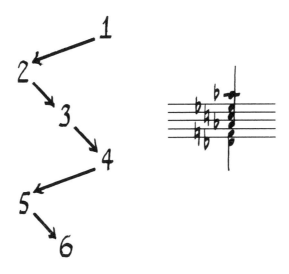

(This case would not apply to two separated chords on the same stave. Here, the third case would apply to each chord):

Never allow a doubt to exist in a player's mind as to which accidental belongs to which note. Take great care that accidentals are written exactly where they belong on the line or space, and are in their proper location ahead of the note.

Chapter 10

SPACING

In theory, a note occupies space in a measure proportionate to its value. This may be best demonstrated in the following chart in 4/4 time:

Notes that are properly spaced:

Are far easier for the player to read than those that have been written in an arbitrary and indiscriminate manner, such as:

A part cannot, and should not, be copied with the same sort of mathematical exactitude as shown on the chart at the beginning of this chapter, for it would result in every measure being of identical length, with too much space allowed for some notes and not enough for others:

The factor determining the length of a measure is the number of notes within it. Consequently, some measures require more space than others, and some half-measures require more space than the other half. The mathematical precision that exists in proper spacing is within each individual measure, and not necessarily in relationship to other measures. In the following example, each measure is of a different length, but observe that a whole note appears to occupy the space of four quarters, a half note the space of two quarters, two quarter notes the space of four eighths, and the dotted quarters the space of three eighths:

With little knowledge or consideration of the way notes should be spaced, the beginning copyist is likely to write parts wherein notes will be out of their proper position, too much space given to some—not enough to others, and is unable to utilize the full length of the stave. Such a poorly written part might appear like the following:

PRACTICE: Copy the preceding example and attempt to space it correctly, keeping in mind that notes occupy space in a measure proportionately to their value. Compare results with the following correctly spaced version:

Just as combinations of dotted half notes and quarter notes are not spaced the same as two half notes, neither are combinations of dotted quarters and eighths spaced the same as two quarters, or combinations of dotted eighths and sixteenths spaced the same as two eighths:

The whole note is written at the beginning of a measure, while a whole rest is centered within the measure:

(Although it may seem redundant to add the figure "1" above the whole rest, it is helpful to the player in sight reading, and its use is a generally accepted practice.)

Incorrect placement of whole notes and whole rests:

In traditional practices, the half rest is located in the same place where a half note would be written:

Such a placement of the rest creates a poorly balanced measure. In manuscript writing, the rest is centered between the first and second beats, or between the third and fourth:

All other rests occupy the same space as would a note of equal value:

Rests generally maintain their proper position within the stave regardless of where the accompanying notes are located:

The following placement of rests is incorrect:

An exception to the rule for location of rests exists when beams are involved. In this case, the rests are written in the same area with the notes:

Further exceptions of rest placements exist in divisi parts and drum parts:

(In such instances, each part on the same stave must stand complete in itself.)

The following are incorrect:

Dotted half and dotted quarter rests are not ordinarily used:

(Exceptions exist in 12/8 time.)

If dotted half and dotted quarter rests, such as in the preceeding example, are used in the score, the correct rest notations should be written for the player:

An example of spacing in 6/8:

(3/8, 9/8 and 12/8 are spaced in the same manner.)

When dotted eighth and dotted sixteenth rests are used, they should be spaced in the same manner as notes of equal value:

A common mistake is the failure to properly align the notes within duet parts. Rewrite the following incorrect example correctly, referring to the chart at the beginning of this chapter if necessary:

The same example written correctly:

A major (and justified) complaint by pianists against some copyists is on improperly aligned piano parts such as the following:

PRACTICE: Copy the above example with proper spacing and alignment of parts, then compare it with the following corrected version:

An example of properly spaced tremolandos:

Planning the "lay-out" of a part can only be accomplished by looking further ahead in the score than the portion being copied. A failure to develop such a habit can only result in allowing too much space for the beginning measures of a line and an insufficient amount for those that follow on the same line:

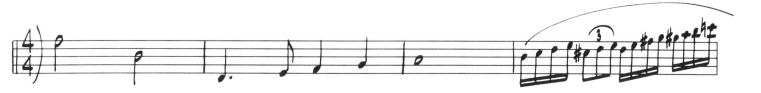

(Such occurrences are referred to as, "getting boxed in". Some copyists "box themselves in" as a matter of course—they consistently "spread" at the beginning of a line, only to be caught short, just as consistently, when they reach the space for the last measure of the line. Getting "boxed in" can only be avoided by knowing in advance of what is coming.)

Correct spacing of the preceding example:

Engravers have the time, and the specialized equipment, to space with mathematical precision within each and every measure. On the other hand, copyists, with the unique nature of their work, must space visually. Lacking the tools and the time at the command of the engraver, a copyist must learn proper spacing through practice, experience and development of the "eye".

Chapter 11
NOTATION

Notation in manuscript writing follows traditional practices with relatively few exceptions.

As the first section of this chapter will deal exclusively with correct notation in 4/4, it is advisable to review the chart on the first page of chapter 10. Notice that other than a whole note and the middle note of half note triplets, that neither notes or beams are carried across the middle of the measure. Further, that except for dotted quarters, quarter note triplets and beams connecting four eighth notes (or combinations of dotted eighths and sixteenths), that neither notes or beams are carried across the quarters of the measure. Other than for these, and the exceptions noted below, these are hard and fast rules:

Variants of the syncopated figure shown in the last measure of the preceding example are in usage today:

The variants just shown are not as acceptable as the figure from which they were derived, and for the sake of clarity, it is better that they be written in accordance to the rule that a note is not carried across the middle of a measure. Therefore, such notes should be divided into two equal parts and tied together across the middle of the measure:

Although it is quite correct to beam groups of three eighth notes together:

For the sake of clarity, it is best that they be written as follows:

The same holds true for this variant:

Although this is correct:

This is preferable:

In dotted eighth and sixteenth combinations, and their variants, the secondary beam must be *within* each group:

The following usages are incorrect:

In traditional writing, the triplet marking (the figure "3"), is not used with any degree of consistency. It is found both under and above notes, and with and without an accompanying slur or bracket.

In order to avoid "eye-jumping", it is best to maintain consistency by always placing the "3" above the notes regardless of stem direction, and further by always using the slur for eighth, sixteenth and thirty-second note triplets, and the bracket for quarter note and half note triplets:

(In all cases, the "3" is always centered over its group.)

The correct number must also be properly centered over groups of five, sixes, sevens, nines, etc. In these cases, the slur is used rather than the bracket:

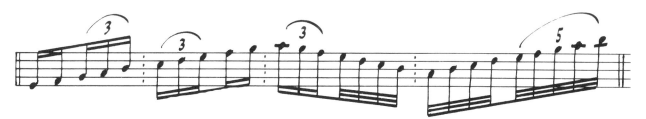

In slow moving tempos, the following notations are correct:

(The same, occurring in fast tempos, are frequently misused, when the true intent was for evenly played groups of fives, sevens and nines.)

In uneven triplets, the "3" is placed over the mathematical center of the group:

Correct exceptions:

Incorrect:

The direction of the slur and/or brace, follows the general direction of the notes in its individual group:

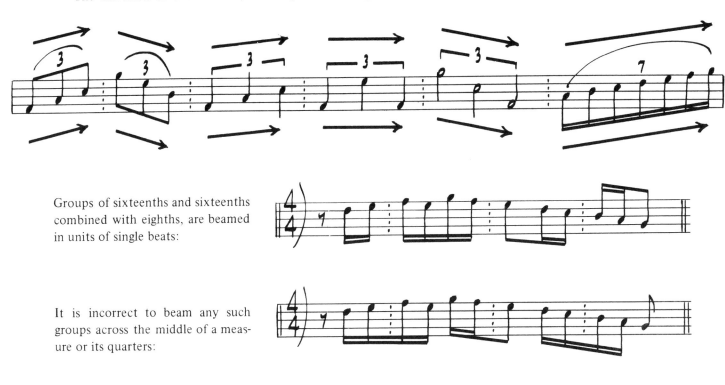

Groups of sixteenths and sixteenths combined with eighths, are beamed in units of single beats:

It is incorrect to beam any such groups across the middle of a measure or its quarters:

"Broken" eighths are correctly beamed and stemmed as follows:

Incorrect:

"Broken" sixteenths are correctly beamed and stemmed as follows:

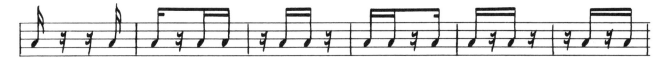

Incorrect:

As already mentioned, groups of three eighths are better written as:

However, groups of three sixteenths should be beamed together:

Incorrect:

Correct notation of dotted sixteenths and thirty-seconds:

Thirty-second note groupings:

Thirty-seconds are sometimes incorrectly written as:

(Not only are the broken secondary beams incorrect, but the addition of the "8" is as superfluous as placing a "4" over a group of four eighths or four sixteenths.)

Examples of incorrect beaming:

Beams must always be used correctly:

(Groups of four eighth notes, four sixteenths, and three eighth note triplets must always be beamed together.)

Rests accompanying single eighth note triplets are correctly written as:

Incorrect:

Providing that each stem can be made of minimum length, groups of notes with wide skips are better beamed as:

Instead of:

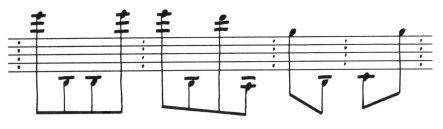

(However, the above stemming is also correct.)

In feeling that broken beaming is an aid to the player in seeing the phrasing, some modern notators give the following as correct:

In actual practice, such beaming can result in confusion, and it is recommended that such phrases be written in traditional form:

On occasion, unusual beaming is used to show intended phrasing:

(Few examples such as the above occur in commercial writing. However, when such do occur, copy exactly as written.)

PRACTICE: Notate the following example correctly:

The previous example correctly notated:

A half rest may not be carried across the middle of a measure:

Incorrect:

Correct:

Quarter and eighth rests are used in such a manner that each and every beat is complete in itself:

Correct: Incorrect:

Rests within quarter note triplet groups:

Correct: Incorrect:

Sixteenth rests are used in such a manner that each half-beat is complete in itself:

Correct: Incorrect:

Double augmentation dots are used in only a few instances:

The above notations are more clear than these:

Incorrect: Correct:

74

Incorrect use of ties will sometimes be encountered in scores:

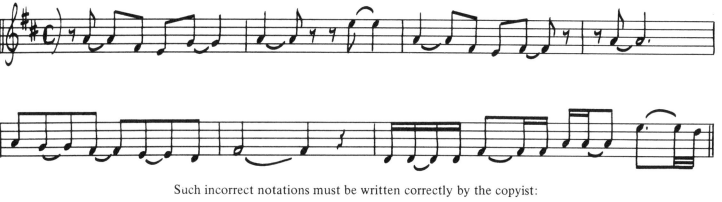

Such incorrect notations must be written correctly by the copyist:

An exception occurs in the following example, where the use of ties is preferable to otherwise correct notations:

Correct:

Preferable:

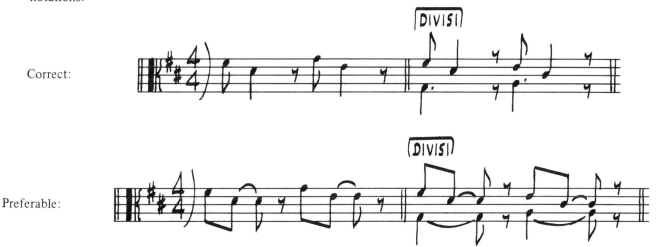

The rules governing notation are so few and simple, that it is difficult to understand how some writers can go so far astray with incorrect notations. Even the self-taught writer should have learned by truly observing printed music he has seen. Incorrect notations are unnecessarily complicated, and often incomprehensible to the player at first glance.

The next example has been made from a collection of incorrect notations which have actually been encountered in scores and copied parts. It is the duty of the copyist to write such notations correctly, for the player cannot be expected to take the time to rewrite his own part even if rehearsal time were not at a premium.

PRACTICE: Rewrite the following example with correct notation. Keep in mind that beams do not cross the middle of a measure, and that with the exception of whole notes, half notes, etc. that neither do notes cross the middle of a measure:

Correct version of the preceding example:

(example continued on next page)

Complex notations become even more complex when notated incorrectly, as can be seen in the following example:

PRACTICE: Write the above example correctly. Keep in mind when writing double time figures such as these that each beat must be complete in itself. Beams do not cross the middle of a measure or its quarters:

Correct version of the preceding example:

NOTATION IN TIME SIGNATURES OTHER THAN 4/4

2/4 is notated exactly as half a measure of 4/4. However, a matter of choice exists in the beaming of eighth notes. It is recommended that each beat be kept separate and complete in itself:

Correct:

Recommended:

(Do not make the mistake of using a half rest in 2/4 writing,—the whole rest is still used.)

Examples of correct notation in 3/4:

The following notations are also correct in 3/4:

However, the following are recommended as being more clear:

(The whole rest is also used in 3/4. Common mistakes are to use a dotted half rest, or a half rest followed by a quarter rest.)

Incorrect example of 3/4 notation:

(example continued on next page)

78

(Observe that several of the measures in the preceding example appear to be written in 6/8. This is a common mistake among self-taught writers, and such errors should be correctly written by the copyist.)

5/4 is notated in one of two different ways:

1) As a 2/4 measure plus one of 3/4:

2) As a 3/4 measure plus one of 2/4:

(The dotted line subdividing the measures in the above examples is not used in 5/4 writing. It has been used here only for clarification. Although one beam connecting six eighth notes was not recommended for 3/4 notation, its use is necessary in 5/4.)

79

Incorrect examples of 5/4 notation:

(Measures must consistently be divided 2+3 or 3+2. The whole rest is used in 5/4—combinations of different rests are incorrect.)

6/4 is also notated in one of two ways:

1)   2/4 + 2/4 + 2/4:

2)   3/4 + 3/4:

(The dots have been used again for clarification—they should not be used in 6/4 writing. Beaming four eighth notes together is correct in the first of the above cases, but not in the second. Six eighth notes are beamed together in the second case, but would create confusion in the first. Whole notes may be used in the first case, but not in the second. A whole rest is recommended for 6/4 writing, although a dotted whole rest is traditional.)

3/2 notation is the same as the first case of 6/4 (2/4 + 2/4 + 2/4):

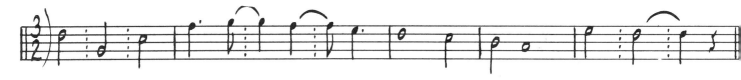

7/4 is notated as a measure of 3/4 plus one of 4/4, or vice versa. A whole rest is still proper, and not combinations of other rests. In actual practice, the dotted bar-lines are sometimes used for added clarity:

3/4 + 4/4:   4/4 + 3/4:

Without the subdivision dots, six successive eighth notes occurring in the 3/4 portion of a 7/4 measure should be beamed together:

With the use of the subdivision dots, six successive eighth notes occurring in the 3/4 portion of the measure should be beamed in separate groups:

7/4 is sometimes written in alternate measures of 3/4 and 4/4, or vice versa. In these cases, a double time signature is used:

Correct notations in 6/8:

81

In analyzing the preceding example, note the following:

1) A "whole" note in 6/8 is a dotted half note, and is not made by tieing two dotted quarters together:

2) Secondary beams are not broken:

3) Primary beams are not broken:

4) The whole rest is still used. It is not a dotted half rest:

5) The correct use of quarter and eighth rests:

6) The following usage of rests is incorrect:

7) Each half of the measure is complete in itself. Notes, beams and rests do not cross the middle of the measure. The following are incorrect:

8) Dotted quarter rests are not used:

9) 6/8 is not notated as 3/4:

(Such incorrect notations occurring in a score must be written correctly for the player):

3/8 — Notation is the same as for half a measure of 6/8. The whole rest is still the same:

9/8 — Notation is the same as for three consecutive measure of 3/8. Beams and rests must conform. Each one-third of the bar is complete in itself, with the exception of a "whole" note—this being a dotted half tied to a dotted quarter:

(Once again, the broken bar-line has been added for clarity—it is not used in 9/8 notation.)

12/8 —Notation is the same as for two consecutive measures of 6/8. The whole rest is still used, although a dotted whole rest is traditional. Dotted quarter rests and dotted half rests may be used in 12/8 as an exception to the general rule:

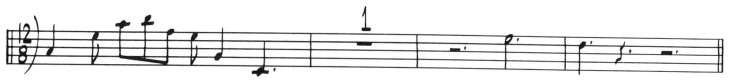

Incorrect notation in 12/8:

The same written correctly:

Rarely seen is the following double time signature:

Chapter 12
PHRASING

Most music is written in phrases of even-numbered measures. Popular music is largely in eight-measure phrases, with inner phrases of two or four measures.

The copyist can aid the player by keeping inner phrases on the same line, rather than in overlapping them from one line to the next. This can be accomplished by adopting a general standard of writing four measures to the line. This helps in keeping the beginning of phrases at the beginning or middle of a line:

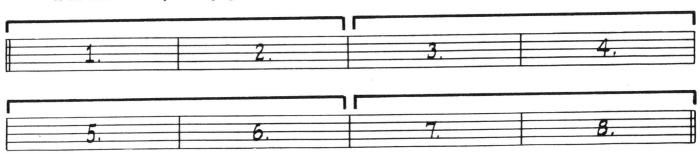

Multiple bar rests will frequently throw a part off balance, but by using half a line for an even-numbered rest, and the space of one measure for odd-numbered rests, balance can be regained:

The proper spacing of multiple bar rests can avoid lopsided phrasing such as:

Another example of
lopsided phrasing:

Lopsided phrasing results in giving the player disconnected phrases, unnecessarily tied-over notes, and overlapping first endings:

Correct phrasing of the preceding example:

When thrown off balance by three-measure endings, it can be quickly regained by writing one line of three measures:

Although it is preferable to start a repeat section at the beginning of a line, on occasion it is necessary to place it in the middle of a line. In such a case, a loss of balance caused by three-measure endings could be regained as in the following example:

An alternative to the same situation:

A repeat sign in the middle of a line causes no problems in regaining balance when two-measure endings are involved:

Writing four measures to the line is only a general standard. Exceptions, in addition to those already noted, would be such as in the following cases:

1) Long passages of whole notes in 4/4 which would be written six or eight measures to the line.
2) Simple 3/4—six measures to the line.
3) Simple 2/4—six or eight measures to the line.
4) 3/8—six or eight measures to the line.

> (Odd numbers of measures per line are avoided as much as possible. An exception would be two successive lines of five measures each, but only as a means of regaining balance.)

Complicated double time passages create another exception, for it becomes necessary to write these three measures to the line, and for overly involved ones, two measures per line. It is better to write these in a readable fashion, rather than attempting to maintain phrasing and crowding the notes too closely together.

As stated earlier in this chapter, improperly spaced multiple bar rests can throw a part off balance; when properly used, they are in an aid in maintaining it. In general, but not always, an even-numbered multiple bar rest occupies the space of two measures, while an odd-numbered one occupies the space of one measure.

The following extended example, made up largely of multiple bar rests, demonstrates how balance can be maintained, and lopsided phrasing avoided, by their proper use.

The two-measure introduction has been indented in order to start the first major phrase at the beginning of a line. (A three-bar intro would also have been indented, while a four bar one would have occupied the entire line. A five-measure intro would have started with an indented two-measure line and finished with three measures covering the entire second line. A six-bar intro, an indented two plus four, and a seven-bar intro as an indented three plus four):

(Example continued on next page)

88

A further example showing the occasional necessity of writing an even-numbered multiple bar rest in the space of one measure instead of two:

A similar example, wherein an odd-numbered multiple bar rest occupies the space of two measures instead of one, while even-numbered ones occupy the space of one measure:

Copyists who ignore proper phrasing make flagrant misuses of multiple bar rests, giving players four and five page parts which could have been properly written on two. The following is an excerpt of such a part:

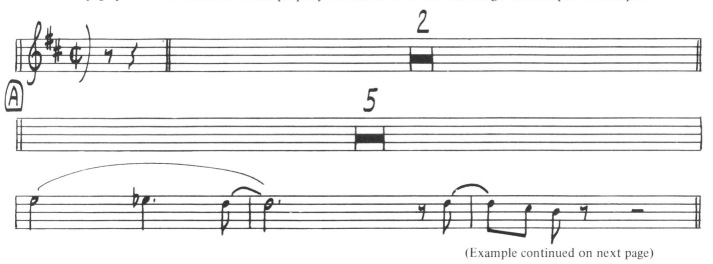

(Example continued on next page)

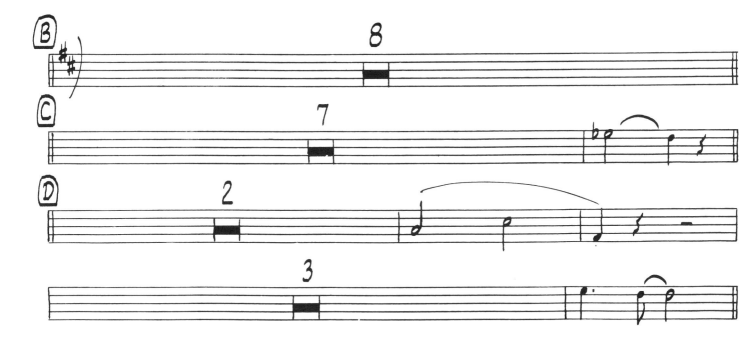

(Unfortunately, there are some professional copyists who consistently write lopsided parts. This is not only an inconvenience to the player, but costs the copyist time as well, for an improperly balanced part consumes more writing time than does a balanced one.)

The discussion thus far has centered around eight-measure phrases. It goes without saying, that any even-numbered phrase (4, 6, 10, 12) would be handled in the same manner.

Also encountered are phrases containing odd numbers of measures. These are no more difficult to handle than are even-numbered ones.

Whereas the basic treatment of the eight-measure phrase is:

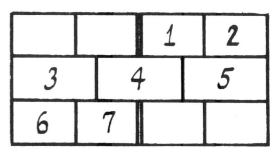

or:

A seven-measure phrase is written as:

or:

A nine-measure phrase as:

1	2	3	4
5	6	7
8	9		

or:

		1	2
3	4	5
6	7	8	9

Taking into consideration the inner phrasing, an alternative to a nine-measure phrase would be:

1	2	3
4	5	6	7
8	9		

or:

		1	2
3	4	5	6
7	8	9

Two successive nine-measure phrases would be handled as:

1	2	3	4
5	6	7
8	9	1	2
3	4	5	6
7	8	9

An eleven-bar phrase, or intermixed odd and even phrases, create no additional problems, for they are handled as combinations of the various layouts already discussed.

Multiple bar rests can always be used to advantage in keeping a part properly phrased. The major decision is whether to allow the space of one or two measures, on occasion, three, or on a rare occasion, the space of an entire line.

Chapter 13
EDITING

It is the fullest obligation of the copyist to edit the score while extracting the individual parts from it. This means being constantly on the alert for the arranger's errors, no matter for what reason they happen. Incorrect rhythmic notations, missing rests, empty measures, wrong instrumentation on "come sopras" (the latter a common mishap), are only a few of the gremlins that pop up; the copyist is the last defender at the walls before the music is given to the players.

More often than not, the professional arranger writes in haste under the pressure of meeting a deadline (which is sometimes of his own making, unfortunately). An alert, knowledgeable and, most of all, conscientious copyist is the best friend an arranger has, for each mistake detected and corrected beforehand will save rehearsal time and contribute to an improved performance.

Regretfully, there are copyists who do not believe they should edit, but feel theirs is a purely mechanical function: The verbatim transfer to paper of a part from a score, no matter what the discrepancies in the original. Luckily, they are few in number, but if it can be said, they may have chosen the wrong profession inasmuch as they serve only to denigrate it.

Sloppy and ineptly written scores have always been the copyist's burden (look through the archives of the masters), but his philosophy must remain such that he has a feeling of fulfillment when he unravels a mystery on the spur of the moment.

PRACTICE: Recopy and edit the following example. The incorrect notations are the same as will be frequently encountered in scores—some are obvious, others hidden. In the practice of copying, one must always keep the key signature in mind—many mistakes will be caught that escape the day-dreamer, or the person who copies by rote. Concentrate on correct beaming and spacing:

(Example continued on next page)

Correct version of the preceding example:

(Example continued on next page)

(Example continued on next page)

OTHER ASPECTS OF EDITING

Accidentals are often used indiscriminately. In the following example, are there missing naturals, or was an accidental from the signature carelessly restated? When such instances are encountered in the score, check the harmony, and/or the other parts:

Any incorrect use of accidentals:

Must be written correctly for the player:

The following passage should arouse the suspicion of the copyist as to the possibility of missing accidentals:

In such an event, check the harmony and/or other parts, and write correctly:

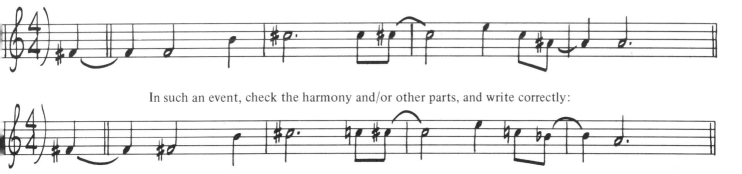

95

In the following instance:

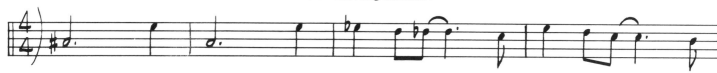

"Courtesy accidentals" should be added to the part by the copyist even though they did not appear on the score:

(In such instances, don't guess. Always check the harmony to determine if a different accidental is missing, or if a "courtesy accidental" is called for.)

Courtesy accidentals are written by most arrangers, however, always be on the lookout for missing ones. Add them to the part if it is felt that their omission would create a doubt in the mind of the player:

Be extremely careful with scores from arrangers who have the bad habit of writing in many (but not all) accidentals that are in the key signature:

An accidental in one octave does not affect the same note in a different octave. The unmarked "C's" in the following example are automatically naturals:

(For safety's sake, naturals should be written before the notes in the other octaves. However, such notes should be carefully checked to see if a sharp was intended. Some arrangers and players mistakenly believe that in such instances the sharp used is good for all other octaves even though the notes are unmarked. Always mark such notes correctly—leave no doubt.)

On occasion, there will be too many beats in a measure:

Is a beam missing, or was the same note accidentally written twice? Check the other parts, it might be any of the following:

Also encountered are measures with insufficient beats:

Check the other parts—it could be either of the following:

Another example of too many beats:

Check the other parts. It might be either of these:

Notes of doubtful location should be checked against the harmony and/or other parts. Never guess at their location, or worse, duplicate them on the part, leaving the responsibility of figuring them out to the player:

A divisi part moving to a unison might appear on a score as:

In such instances, use stems—up, stems—down instead of single stems:

Although the following example would be correct for piano, as an accidental once stated, affects all similiar notes within the same measure, this is incorrect for divisi writing, where each part must be complete in itself:

The same example written correctly as a divisi part:

Avoid duplicating on the part the following common score error:

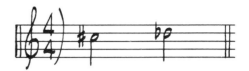

Tremolos and tremulants must always be written correctly. Incorrect variants, as those that follow, must not be written for the player:

Certain instruments (notably violas and cellos) will have passages written in a combination of clefs:

A passage, such as the above, can be improved for the player. One must also be certain that the player is given the proper return to his natural clef:

Abbreviations such as the following are often used in the score:

These may not be written for the player. Always write them out in full:

It is important to know the habits and intentions of the arranger. When the following abbreviation is seen on a score:

Which of the following did he intend?:

98

If this abbreviation is found on a score:

Tremolos might have been intended, but then again, the arranger might have meant:

Half measure repeats used in the score:

May not be given to the player. Copy out in full:

Passages containing indiscriminate uses of the "8va" symbol:

Must be written correctly for the player:

When a sequential pattern begins on a score:

The pattern should first be written in full on the part. Once the pattern is established, abbreviations are permissable as long as no changes occur in the basic sequence. The direction "simile" should also be given: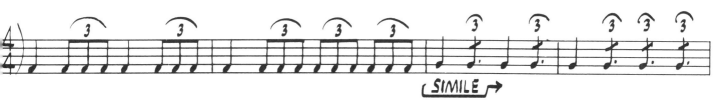

(Observe the recommended triplet abbreviation.)

99

Although single beat repeats are used with regularity in symphonic writing, they are best avoided in commercial copying. They will occur on scores, as abbreviations, in a variety of ways:

As an exception, they are sometimes used as abbreviations for simple figurations on piano and harp parts, but even in this case it is not often advisable to do so. If used, a single slash mark is the accepted abbreviation:

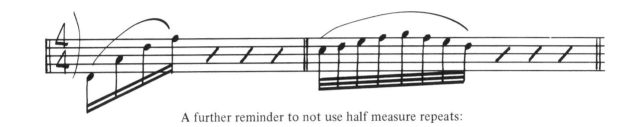

A further reminder to not use half measure repeats:

(Write the notes out in full for the player.)

Three or four measure repeat signs are incorrect:

When such abbreviations occur on the score, the passage must be written out in its entirety for the player:

A four or eight measure phrase is on occasion repeated many times. Repeat signs are used, and the number of times the phrase is to be played is clearly marked:

If the passage is to be played more than four times, the passage should be rewritten and marked with an additional direction. If the passage is to be played five times–write the pattern twice (both with a set of repeat signs)–mark the first passage "Play 3 x's", and the second "Play 2 x's".

Six Times–Write Twice (3 + 3)
Seven Times–Write Twice (4 + 3)
Eight Times–Write Twice (4 + 4)
Nine Times–Write Three Times (3 + 3 + 3)
etc., etc.

Single measure repeat signs are used with regularity, but for the sake of the player, write no more than a total of eight measures to the line. Further, the measures should be counted for the player by placing numerals directly over the repeat sign:

Always consider the problems of the player. Imagine his plight if he were confronted with the following flagrant misuse of single measure repeat signs:

In the event the measure is to be played more than eight times, the measure should be rewritten at the beginning of the next line before continuing use of the repeat sign. For a total of ten measures, the spacing would be six measures on the first line and four on the second.

12 measures–write twice (6+6)
14 measures–write twice (8+6)
16 measures–write twice (8+8)
18 measures–write three times (6+6+6)
20 measures–write three times (8+6+6)
etc., etc.

To maintain balance with the occurrence of an odd-number of single measure repeat signs:

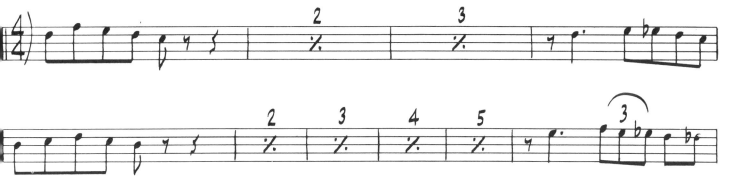

Or as in the following example, where the odd-numbered measure has been rewritten at the beginning of the next line:

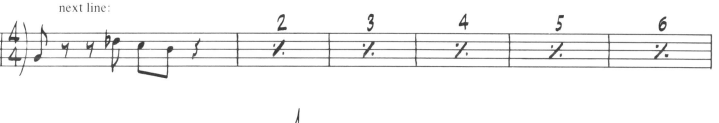

A typical abbreviation found on scores which should not be used on the copied part:

Write the notes out in full, making correct use of ties:

It is obvious that single measure repeats should never be used as in the following example:

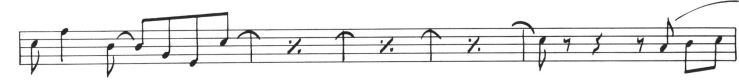

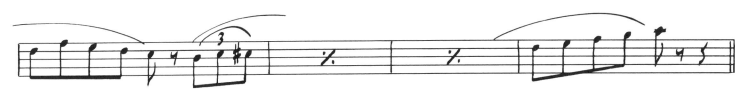

(Although much additional work is involved, it is essential that passages such as these be written out in full.)

Never begin a new line with a single measure repeat:

(Such a usage forces the player's eyes to jump, and could be responsible for him losing his place.)

Two measure repeats: As in the case of single measure repeats, never give a player a total of more than eight measures per line:

Once again, imagine the plight of the player when confronted with the likes of the following:

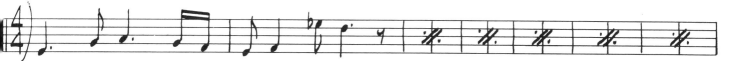

(When there are a total of ten or more measures, the spacing should be handled in the same manner as the case of single measure repeats.)

Two measure repeats should not be used as in the following manner:

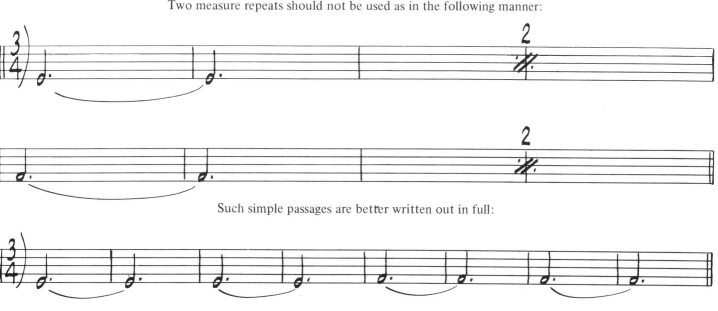

Such simple passages are better written out in full:

Two measure repeats used in unbalanced phrases are potential trouble makers:

Two measure repeats are best used when the return is to the beginning of a line:

Never begin a line with a two measure repeat. If the abbreviation cannot be used in its proper place, the phrase should be rewritten:

The abbreviation should especially never be used in this manner:

Although the following may occur in a score (from the last measure of one page to the first measure of the next), it should certainly not be used for the player:

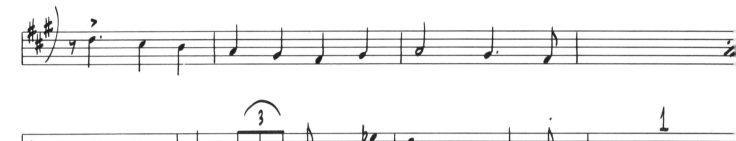

An arranger's "short—cut" that may never be used for the player:

The next example shows a common misuse of the two measure repeat:

The above example can only be written properly with single measure repeats:

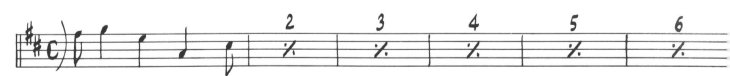

Another common misuse:

Such occurrences must be written correctly:

Never break up a multiple bar rest just in order to use a two measure repeat:

The multiple bar rest must be used correctly, and the repeated measure written out in full:

An example of a part being thrown out of balance by incorrect phrasing:

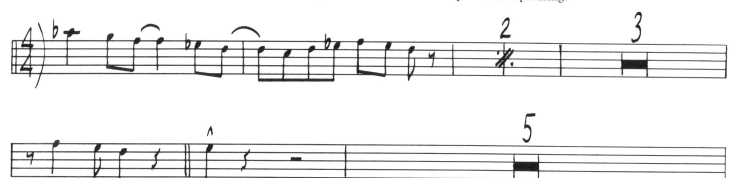

The same example phrased properly:

Some arrangers count and mark multiple bar rests on the score as a courtesy to the copyist:

Let a word to the wise be sufficient:

Chapter 14
ENGLISH ON PARTS

All directions written on parts must be clearly marked and completely legible. Rehearsal letters, and most directions, are placed above the stave and "boxed". A certain few directions are placed below the stave and are preferably underlined. The following example shows proper placement of English on a part, and further demonstrates the correct way of indicating instrument changes:

(It should be kept in mind the woodwind player needs as much advance notice of instrument changes as possible.)

In traditional practices, instrument changes are written as follows:

PRACTICE: Rewrite the preceding example—give the player advance notice of instrument changes, box the directions and rehearsal letters, use double bars at rehearsal letters, and use a red pencil to arc the key changes. There is more clarity in a manuscript part thus written than in one done according to traditional practices.

Brass players must be given advance notice of mute changes:

Mute changes as indicated traditionally:

Instrument changes as written for pianists:

Instrument changes as written for percussionists:

Mute changes for string players may be indicated in musical terms:

Or translated:

Examples of the types of directions (with recommended abbreviations) that should be placed above the line and boxed:

| TO ALTO | | TO TENOR | | TO BARI. | | TO CLAR. | | TO E♭ CLAR. | | TO PICCOLO |

| TO FLUTE | | TO ALTO FLUTE | | TO BASS FLUTE | | TO OBOE | | TO ENG. HORN |

| TO BASS CLAR. | | TO E♭ CONTRA BASS CLAR. | | TO B♭ CONTRA BASS CLAR. |

| TO BASSOON | | TO CONTRA BASSOON | | TO FLÜGEL | | TO TRPT. | | TO TUBA |

| TO VALVE TROM. | | TO BASS TROM. | | TO TYMPS | | TO BELLS | | TO XYLO |

| TO VIBES | | MOTOR ON | | MOTOR OFF | | HARD MALLETS | | TO PIATTI |

| TO BANJO | | TO CELESTE | | TO ORGAN | | BLEND W/SXS | | BLEND W/TROMS |

| CUP | | HARMON | | ST. MUTE | | SOLOTONE | | BUCKET | | OPEN | | Q.H. |

| HAND IN BELL | | PLGR. | | IN STAND | | PIZZ | | ARCO | | SPICC. | | DETACHÉ |

| COL LEGNO | | SORDS. | | SENZA SORDS. | | SLOWLY | | FAST- IN 2 | | IN 1 |

| IN 3 | | IN 4 | | MAESTOSO | | ALLEGRO | | ANDANTE | | PIU MOSSO | | ROCK |

| MODTO | | RUBATO | | NO VIB. | | W/VIB. | | SOLO AD LIB | | END OF SOLO |

| SOLI | | TEMPO I° | ETC.

("W/" is the acceptable abbreviation for "with". "W/HORN" indicates that the player is to blend his part with the horn. "Q. H." is the accepted abbreviation for "quasi horn".)

The following abbreviations should be avoided:

RUB. ATO A.T. S. MT. CUP M. HARM. Q.H'N. OP.

N.V. TO VIB TO VIBS TO CL. TO B.CL. TO C.B. CL.

TO FL. TO AL. FL. TO AL. SX. TO TNR. SX. TO BARY

TO BS. BONE TO CEL. TO PNO. H.I.B. DIM. ACC.

When making instrument changes, it is not necessary to state the "key" of the following instruments:

TO "C" FLUTE   TO "G" FLUTE   TO B♭ CLAR.   TO B♭ BASS CLAR.

TO E♭ ALTO SAX   TO B♭ TENOR SAX   TO E♭ BARITONE SAX

Examples of the type of directions written below the stave and underlined:

DIMIN.   CRESC.   ACCELL.   RALL.   RIT.   CRESC. POCO A POCO

Chapter 15
TRANSPOSITION

A copyist must be able to transpose from any given key to all other keys, not only within the same clef, but also from within one clef to any other. Much more is required than merely transposing parts for "E-flat" and "B-flat" instruments from a score written in concert key.

Frequently the copyist is directed to recopy a previous section in a different key. The commonest transpositions are half and full tones, either up or down.

Recording arrangements are often converted from their original instrumentation to one that will fit the requirements of a night club orchestra. Some typical transpositions: alto flute to clarinet, violas and/or cellos to clarinets and/or bass clarinets, bassoon to bass clarinet, french horns to flugelhorns or trombones.

On occasion, an entire score must be recopied in a different key. Although a transposed score presents few problems, consider the various transpositions that are called for if the score were in concert.

Original arrangements from Broadway shows are sometimes transposed for singers doing summer stock. Think of the problems of transposing from "A" to "D-flat" (the latter key being more advisable for players than "C-sharp"), and the reverse transposition "D-flat" to "A".

The preparation of conductor parts from transposed scores requires "reverse" transpositions to the concert key.

Some arrangers avoid writing in the key of "B", and instead use the key of "B-flat", and ask the copyist to do the necessary transposition. Obviously, problems will arise in both transposed and concert scores.

In working from a concert score in the key of "B":
  1)   Alto and baritone saxes must be written in the key of "A-flat".
  2)   Tenor saxes and trumpets should be written in "D-flat" instead of "C-sharp".

In working from a concert score in the key of "E":
  1)   Alto and baritone saxes should be written in "D-flat" instead of "C-sharp".
  2)   Tenor saxes and trumpets should be written in "G-flat" instead of "F-sharp".

When recopying an arrangement in a new key, it is frequently possible to save a few of the original parts: the conductor part may be salvaged, but a notation should be made at the top of the first page stating the key in which the parts are copied . The drum part can also be saved unless it contains notes for bells, xylophone, tympani, or other pitched instruments. As most singers read by relative pitch, vocal and choir parts can also be saved—however, if any of the singers have perfect pitch, it will become necessary to recopy these parts in the new key.

The importance of having facility in transposition can be demonstrated by the following example, wherein the copyist is directed to construct a piano part from the instrumental lines on a transposed score:

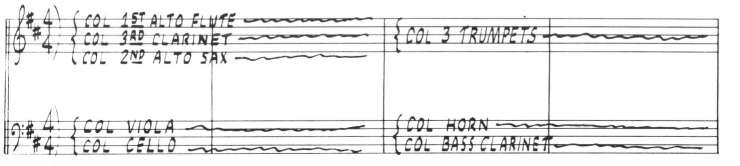

Chapter 16
PREPARING A SCORE AND PARTS FOR COPYING

First, check the score pages to make sure they are in proper order. Arrangements have been copied with two or more reversed score pages.

Next, go through the score, and with a red pencil draw double bars at each rehearsal letter, key change, time signature change, rubato, a tempo, etc. If the score carries numbered bars instead of rehearsal letters, draw a double bar at the beginning of each major phrase.

A properly marked score, eases the job of copying. The red double bar enables one to see the phrases at a glance, and aids in making plans for well layed out parts. It also serves as a reminder not to carelessly omit directions and signature changes which may have been written only at the top of the score page. Without the use of the double bar, such omissions are frequent occurrences, especially on the parts written on the lower lines of the score page.

If the arranger is one who writes directions at the middle or bottom of a score page, the directions should be added in red at the top of various pages as the score is being prepared.

Some arrangers write dynamics and accents only on the lead part of a section. If the lead switches to one of the inner parts, the markings become buried in the middle of the section. With the red pencil, mark these dynamics and accents in order that they will be noticed when copying other parts in the section. In trusting to luck to remember such marking can only result in no two parts being marked the same.

Always take the extra time to prepare a score properly, for any omissions of markings or directions are as much mistakes as wrong notes. A good copyist is an accurate one.

The failure to double bar a score can result in writing a 32 bar rest for a player, when he should have been informed of the changes and directions that occurred within that section:

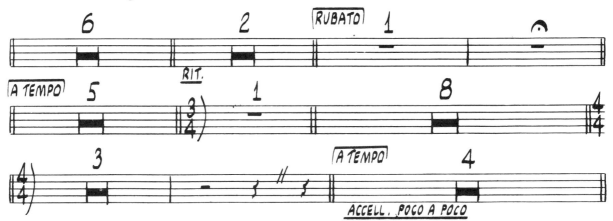

The length of an arrangement determines whether a "D.S." written in the score may be used on the parts or if the section must be copied out in full. A player cannot be expected to "D.S." from page 4 of his part back to page 1, play a few measures, then jump to page 5. The average music stand can accommodate three pages of music opened out—it therefore follows, that if the coda cannot be placed on the third page that the "D.S." cannot be used, and the entire section be copied out in full. If bar numbers had been used on the score in such a case, the copyist should continue the numbers in sequence throughout the "D.S." section, then renumber the measures in the coda.

> (In writing an average of four measures per line, 112 measures of continuous playing is
> the longest a single line part may be to be written on three pages—the title occupies two
> of the thirty lines, so a total of 28 lines x 4 remains for the actual part. Multiple bar
> rests allow more leeway, but in general, be extremely cautious of using a "D.S." on
> single line parts which are longer than 112 measures.)

Once the score has been properly prepared, a part for each instrument in the orchestra should be titled, either by hand or with the use of rubber stamps. In titling by hand, the copying pen is used for headings, and the speedball pen for the title of the selection. The name of the instrument is placed in the upper left hand corner, and that of the artist in the upper right hand corner. An added nicety is to add the name of the arranger.

Titles on 10–10 manuscript paper:

1ST TRUMPET

PEGGY LEE

ARR. by MUNDELL LOWE

IT'S HIGH TIME

4th TROMBONE

Arranged By
JACK FASCINATO

ERNIE FORD

IT'S HIGH TIME

Titles on 8–10 manuscript paper:

3RD TENOR SAX

NANCY WILSON

ARR by JIMMY JONES

IT'S HIGH TIME

1st TRUMPET

Arranged By
BENNY CARTER

PEGGY LEE

IT'S HIGH TIME

CLUB ARRANGEMENT

(If an artist has more than one arrangement of the same song, it should carry an additional marking as the one above, or marked "-2-" as in the case below.)

Titles on custom printed title paper:

2ND TROMBONE

MATT MONRO
ARR by SID FELLER

It's High Time
– 2 –

2nd ALTO SAX

Arranged By
VAN ALEXANDER

Dean Martin Show

IT'S HIGH TIME

Woodwind parts should be numbered consecutively, the number followed by the name of the instrument the player starts on at the beginning of the arrangement:

> 1st Piccolo
> 2nd Flute
> 3rd Alto Sax
> 4th Tenor Sax
> 5th Baritone Sax

Guitar parts should also be titled with the starting instrument, such as "Electric Guitar", "Acoustical Guitar", "Electric Rhythm Guitar", etc.

The rhythm drum part is titled "Drums". Additional drum parts as: "1st Percussion", "2nd Percussion", etc.

Once a score has been completely copied, it is to be bound together in book form. The blank side of the first page should be fully titled—this page will act as the cover of the bound score:

IT'S HIGH TIME

CLUB ARRANGEMENT

NANCY WILSON

Arranged By
OLIVER NELSON

To bind the score—working with the pages face up, tape pages together a few at a time, using half-inch masking tape:

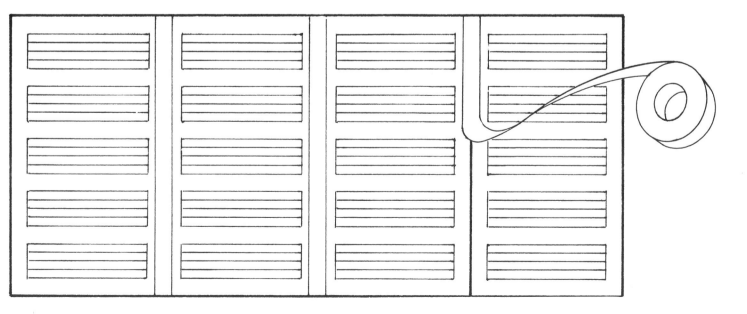

Continue by folding the completed pages "accordion" style, and continue binding and folding until complete:

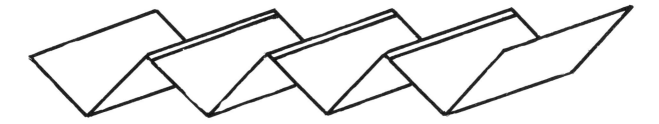

Once the score is completely bound, the left edge should be "backed" with inch or inch-and-a-half masking tape, thereby completing the "book":

It is not advisable to put a score together with punched holes and string.

Orchestra parts of more than two pages must also be taped together. Use a full length piece of tape on the reverse side of the paper.

Chapter 17
COPYING AN ORCHESTRA PART

With a thorough knowledge of the principles of notation, spacing, balance and phrasing, woodwind, brass and bass parts should present no problems. Preparation of such parts entails only "straight ahead" copying.

> (String, drum, guitar, harp, piano, vocal, choir and conductor parts will be treated separately in following chapters.)

An obsolescent practice, is the "carrying" of clefs and key signatures; that is, both are restated at the beginning of each line of a part. Today's player is more than capable of remembering the key he is in. However, as a reminder to the player, the key should be restated at the beginning of each new page, and a clef at the beginning of each line if the player is in a clef other than his normal one.

Concentrate on staying on the correct line of the score when copying—use a straight-edge placed below the line of the score being copied if necessary. Lack of concentration frequently results in copying a few notes or measures from an adjacent line. Such mistakes become disastrous at rehearsals.

The chances of copying from the wrong line are increased when working from score paper with continuous bar-lines:

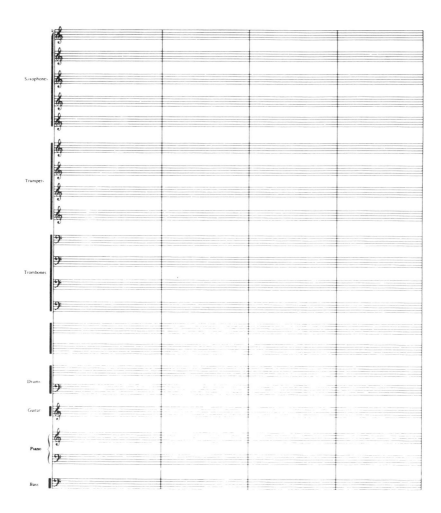

> (On score paper such as the above, it is wise to draw red horizontal lines separating the sections. Here again, a straight-edge placed under the line being copied is helpful.)

115

Score paper with broken bar-lines between sections is an aid to the copyist in maintaining his place on the score:

Page turns: In long arrangements, one must give advance consideration to where the player can turn pages. As three pages can be accommodated on the average music stand, turns must exist on page 3, and on each succeeding odd-numbered page. In order to accomplish this, it becomes necessary to look ahead in the score to find a suitable multiple bar rest to use for the turn. On occasion, only a few lines of the third page may be written on, for another multiple bar rest may not occur for another ten or twelve lines. At other times it may be necessary to write a few lines consisting of five or more measures each in order to reach a multiple bar rest. Bass, guitar and drum parts present problems in long arrangements, for the players are most often working continuously. Simple guitar and bass parts may have to be written six measures per line in such cases.

The indication for a page turn is "V.S." (Volti subito):

The tempo is a deciding factor in how many bars rest the player will need to make a page turn.

A basic knowledge of woodwind fingerings is essential. On occasion it becomes necessary to have the player make a page turn with his right hand while holding a sustained note with his left hand.

Page turns are especially important for string players. With two players reading from each stand, half the string section will be forced to drop out to turn pages if sufficient rest measures are not provided for the purpose.

The use of dal segnos demand a well layed out part. The necessary boxing should be in red:

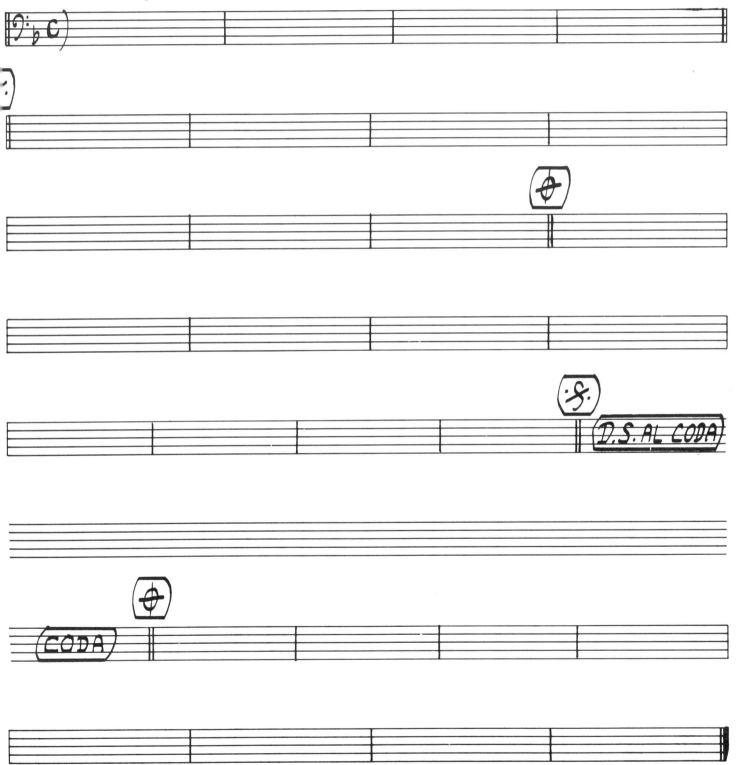

(It is preferable to have the sign at the beginning of a line; also preferable is the use of indentations and a blank line separating the main body of the part from the coda.)

An improper layout, unboxed signs, lack of indentations and the failure to leave a blank line between the main body and the coda, are hindrances to the player:

The copyist should assume responsibility for giving the player the necessary key reminders:

A da capo (return to the beginning of the piece) is written and spaced as the dal segno. The abbreviation "D.C." is used instead of "D.S.":

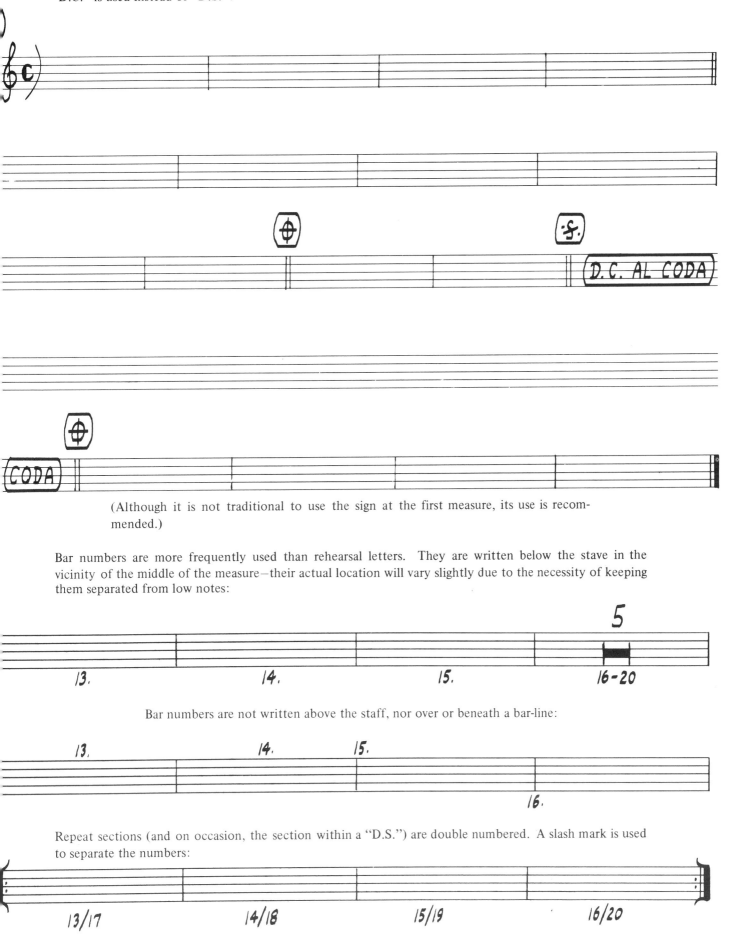

(Although it is not traditional to use the sign at the first measure, its use is recommended.)

Bar numbers are more frequently used than rehearsal letters. They are written below the stave in the vicinity of the middle of the measure—their actual location will vary slightly due to the necessity of keeping them separated from low notes:

Bar numbers are not written above the staff, nor over or beneath a bar-line:

Repeat sections (and on occasion, the section within a "D.S.") are double numbered. A slash mark is used to separate the numbers:

Following a long series of rests, the copyist should assume the responsibility of giving the player a cue before his next entrance. Cues are written with small notes, stems–up or stems–down, depending upon the register of the cue. Whole measure rests must be included in each measure of the cue section. Cue notes must conform to the transposition of the player's instrument:

An example of a cue with stems–up:

An example of a cue with stems–down:

The instrumentalist should be given proper notice of the beginning and end of ad lib solos:

When both melody and chord symbols are given the soloist, the chord symbols must be properly located above the notes:

A dashed line is used to indicate the length of short solos:

The dashed line is also used for short ad lib fills:

The use of the electric eraser to remove ink smudges may also remove the lines of the stave. The lines may be redrawn with a sharply pointed soft lead pencil and the straight-edge. The slovenly copyist seldom takes the time to redraw the erased lines and leaves it to the player to figure out the notes:

The "ultra-slovenly" have been known to cross out mistakes, leaving behind a messy and hard-to-read part:

(There can be no excuse for this type of work.)

All mistakes detected in the score should be marked *on the score* in ink, and if time permits, to discuss these with the arranger prior to the rehearsal.

Be alert for omissions in the score. For example, if the 3rd and 4th trombones have several blank measures while the other two trombones and trumpets are playing, it is possible that the arranger had a lapse and forgot to fill in the parts. In such a case, check with the arranger. Do not attempt to fill in the missing parts unless you are positive that rests were not intended, and you are completely familiar with the arranger's style of voicing. Be certain to mark any such additions on the score in ink.

Single measure repeat signs are frequently missing on drum parts on the score. Never be guilty of writing rests on the part without bothering to check the omission against the other rhythm parts.

Many mistakes and omissions on a score are obvious, while others can be well hidden. In becoming familiar with the habits and idiosyncracies of individual arrangers, even the well-hidden errors will become apparent.

Music for night club comedians must be well layed out for the player. Study the part on the following page and observe the type of information that is necessary, and how it is written on the part. The instrumentalists require only an occasional "word cue", however, *all* such cues must be written on the piano and conductor parts:

BOWS

Chapter 18
DRUM PARTS

The simplest drum part written by arrangers is one that gives the player only an indication of when and when not to play—the drummer is given complete freedom to improvise. Hash marks are used in place of notes. and "English" used to indicate different rhythm patterns:

Slightly less sketchy, is the part that gives the player a little more information, but still allows room for improvisation. Only basic rhythm patterns are indicated, along with an occasional accent that the arranger definitely desires:

The first space of the stave is used for the bass drum, the third space for the snare drum, and the fourth space for cymbals and high-hat, with an "x" being used in place of the conventional note-head for any of the various cymbals. The fourth space is also used for tom toms, temple blocks, cow bells, wood blocks, etc. However, an "English" notation is written directly over the notes affected in these cases:

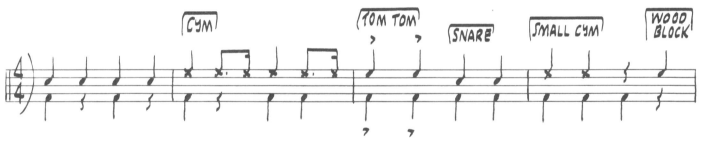

When more than one tom tom is used, it becomes necessary to indicate pitches from the lowest to the highest. The third and fourth spaces, as well as the space above the stave, are used. The same three spaces are used in writing for three cymbals of different pitch:

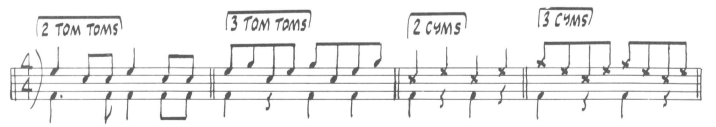

(Temple blocks are notated the same as tom toms, and with the proper indication.)

Using the three suggested spaces is better than using the second, third and fourth spaces, where clutter would be the result:

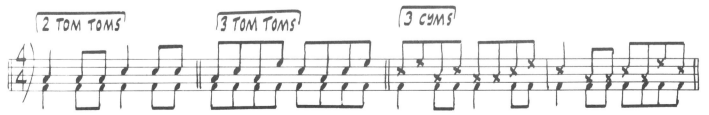

(It should be noted that because of the extra space required for drum parts, stems must sometimes be shorter than minimum length.)

In essence, the drum part is the same as a duet part. Both parts on the stave must be correctly aligned:

An incorrect and inconsiderate example:

Rests must be used properly in order that both parts are complete in themselves:

Incorrect:

An exception to omitting rests exists in the so called "three-line" drum part. If written correctly, the arranger's intent is obvious. Any attempt on the part of the copyist to include the missing rests would result in needless clutter:

In writing for cymbals, diamond shaped note-heads are used for half and whole notes:

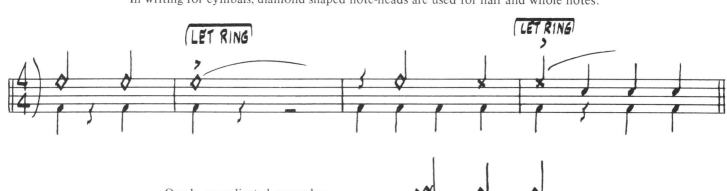

Overly complicated examples:

Slash marks should be used on drum parts only
when they apply to both parts:

Incorrect use of slash marks:

Such abbreviations, used on the score
must be written out for the drummer:

Many arrangers like to show the drummer occasional bits of orchestral information. Such indications are
written in the space above the staff:

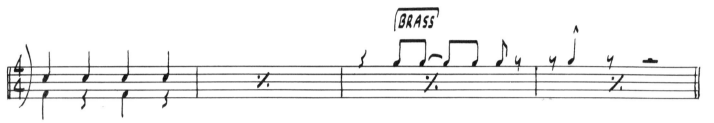

Or it might become necessary for the information to be written like this:

(Ad lib solos and fills will be indicated for the drummer in the same manner as shown
in the previous chapter. Either notes or slash marks are used.)

Only the following abbreviations are recommended:

Snare Drum	— SN. or S.D.
Cymbal	— CYM.
Tom Tom(s)	— TOM(S)
Wood Block	— WD. BLK.
High Hat	— HI HAT
Small Cymbal	— SM. CYM.
Large Cymbal	— LG. CYM.
Suspended Cymbal	— SUS. CYM.
Bass Drum	— B.D.
Triangle	— TRIA.
Temple Blocks	— TEMPLE BLX.
Ride Cymbal	— RIDE CYM.
Tambourine	— TAMB.
Tam Tam	— (No Abbreviation)
Rim Shot	— RIM

(Avoid using abbreviations such as: "CYMB.",
"T.T.", "H.H.", "W.B.", "T.B.", "R.S.", etc.)

125

Devices such as police and slide whistles, when used, should be completely spelled out on the part:

(The written notes have nothing to do with actual pitch. In the case of the slide whistle, they are used only as an indication of low to high sounds.)

Most rhythm drum parts consist mainly of single measure repeats. Consequently, it is very important that these parts be layed out in such a manner that the drummer can take in an entire phrase at a single glance. These parts can generally be spaced eight measures to the line:

126

As it isn't always possible to write a drum part eight measures to the line, any loss of balance should be reacquired as soon as possible. This can best be accomplished by an occasional use of four measures to the line:

(Odd numbers of measures to the line should be avoided except in the case of odd-numbered phrases.)

127

Two bar repeats: These should be used with discretion. No more than a total of eight measures should be written on a line:

There can be no excuse for a spread-out drum part, nor for incorrect usages of the single bar repeat:

The following example is extremely difficult to read. In this poorly layed out part, the sparse, mislocated numbers only add to the general confusion:

If there is more than one drummer in an orchestra, the second one is generally called the "percussionist" or the "utility drummer". He plays the various "mallet" instruments: Xylophone, vibraphone, marimba, bells, chimes, tympani, etc., and in addition is called upon to play tambourine, bongos and other Latin rhythm instruments, as well as many various and sundry percussive devices.

The various instruments in such a "battery" cover much floor space, and the frequent changes of instruments and types of mallets, makes it impossible for him to carry his music around with him. Consequently, such parts are copied on onion skin paper, and copies are printed for each music stand he will be using. The part is titled "Percussion", and would be written as follows:

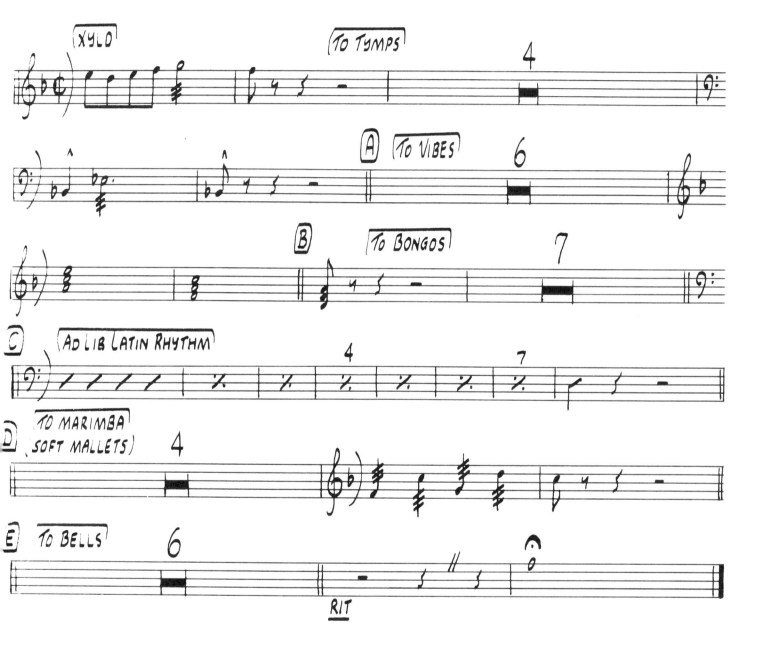

In the example, note the following:

1) As in previously discussed cases, as much advance notice as possible is given for instrument and mallet changes.

2) Other than for tympani, key signatures are used for pitched instruments.

3) Clef and key changes stated at the beginning of a line, were prestated at the end of the preceding one.

4) Tremolos are written for quarter notes, and notes of longer value for xylophone, marimba and tympani. They are not used for accented quarter notes or for notes of lesser value except in slow tempos.

129

Accidentals must be used in each measure of a tympani part, even though the pitch has already been established:

Incorrect:

If there is more than one percussionist in the orchestra, separate onion skin parts are written for each player. The parts are titled "1st Percussion", "2nd Percussion", etc.

In certain instances, the percussion parts are written on one part:

The advantage of such a part is that players can readjust the doubles between themselves if it becomes impossible for one player to make a change in the time allowed. Further, if one part contains more rests than the other, the busier part will act as a cue. Combined parts tend to become quite long, especially when three percussionists are written on the same part. Page turn problems arise and must be dealt with as in chapter 17.

Chapter 19
GUITAR PARTS

Slash marks and chord symbols are more generally used for guitar parts than are fully spelled out chords. Chord symbols must be placed squarely over the mark:

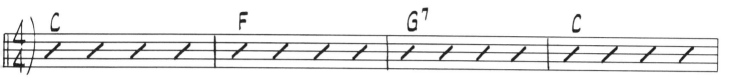

"X" note-heads are not used as a substitute for the slash mark:

Stems are used on slash marks when any deviation from a straight quarter note pattern occurs. In such instances, stems should be used on all notes within the affected measure. The direction of the stem is always down from the mark:

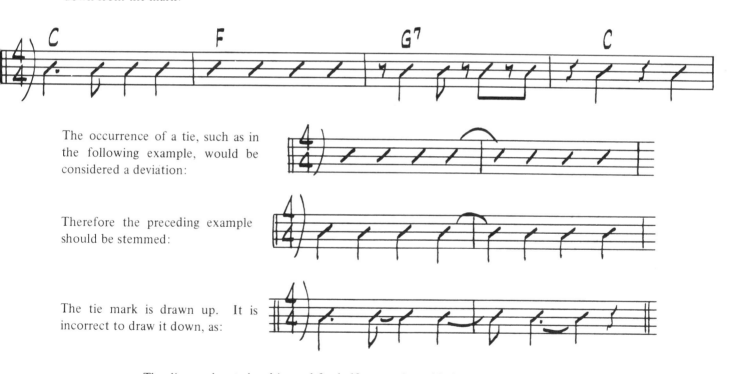

The occurrence of a tie, such as in the following example, would be considered a deviation:

Therefore the preceding example should be stemmed:

The tie mark is drawn up. It is incorrect to draw it down, as:

The diamond note-head is used for half notes, dotted halves, and whole notes:

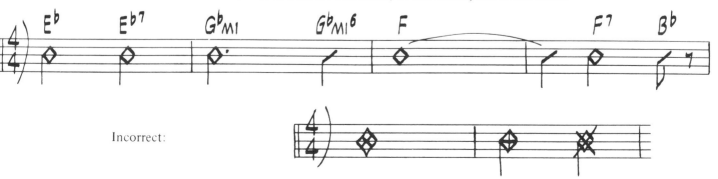

Incorrect:

Arpeggios are indicated with a wavy line before the slash mark. With their occurrence, the mark should be stemmed:

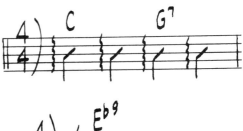

Arpeggios are generally played from the bottom note upwards. A reverse arpeggio is indicated as:

The following variants and/or mixtures of stemmed slash marks combined with unstemmed ones are incorrect:

It is imperative that chord symbols be placed squarely over the marks:

Never be guilty of slovenly practices:

It is always important that the player know exactly where the changes occur, especially in a passage like this:

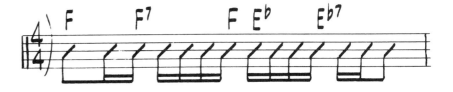

132

In guitar writing, an exception must be made to the location of accents and triplet indications—they are best placed beneath the stems and beneath the stave:

The attempt to place them above the stave results in clutter:

The slovenly copyist often ignores slash marks in straight 4/4 patterns, and writes symbols either above the stave or within it. The player is forced to guess the true location of the changes:

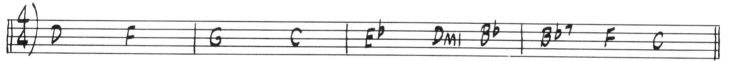

When the arranger writes chord symbols, but at the same time asks for specific top notes to the chords, either of the following notations are acceptable:

A "no tonality" effect is written with "X" note-heads and properly indicated:

Harmonics are indicated with a small "o" placed over the notes:

Particular rhythms are sometimes indicated with "English" as well as with the correctly written rhythmic figures:

Once a rhythm pattern has been established, the direction "simile" may be used:

However, the original pattern should be rewritten at the beginning of each major phrase, and the direction "simile" then restated. Be on guard when using the "simile" indication—do not allow several measures of deviations from the basic pattern slip by, such as the following:

Whoever invented the following system of guitar notation, had a very original idea. However, such writing would be more of a hindrance than an aid to the guitarist:

When   guitarist is asked to accompany a singer, as frequently occurs during rubato passages, he should be give· the proper indication along with the melody and guitar symbols:

It is incorrect to cancel accidentals in chord symbols:

Edit such occurrences and write correctly:

Chord symbols are often misplaced in writing "anticipations":

Symbols must be placed where they properly belong:

A chord symbol should not be carried across a bar-line:

134

In occurrences such as in the preceding example, the symbols should be reiterated:

The following usage is incorrect:

The following indications:

Are better notated as:

Although arrangers will take short cuts in writing chord symbols:

Such abbreviations must not be given to the player. If necessary, study the parts within the score to discover the true intent, and write such occurrences correctly for the guitarist:

135

The direction "col piano right hand" is frequently found on the guitar line of a score, as is the direction "col piano left hand" found on the bass line. The written notes would be where they actually sound:

In preparing the guitar and bass parts, keep in mind that both instruments sound an octave lower than written. Consequently, the notes in the above example would have to be written an octave higher for both the guitar and bass:

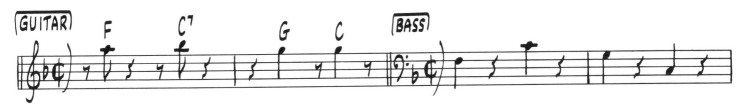

(The reverse octave "transposition" becomes necessary if the piano part is constructed from the guitar and bass lines.)

Examples of correct stemming, flagging and beaming for the guitar:

Virtually every writer of music has his own theory of how chord symbols should be written, and agreement between any two persons is impossible. In feeling that there should be a consistency, conformity and simplification, the chart on the following page is presented as a suggestion for standardization:

CHORD SYMBOLS	DO NOT USE THESE (OR VARIANTS): EDIT THEM WHEN THEY OCCUR ON SCORES.				
G	GMA	GMAJ	Gma	Gmaj	Gmj
G^6	G6TH	G(ADD E)	G(E)		
G^7	G7TH	G(ADD F♮)	G(F)		
GMI	G−	GM	Gm	Gmi	Gmin
GMI^7	G−^{7}	GM^7	Gm^7	Gmi^7	Gmin^7
GMA^7	G✄	GM^7	Gmj^7	G#^{7}	G7# / G7+
GMA^9	GMA$^{7(9)}$	GMA$^{7(ADD A)}$	G✄$^{(9)}$		
G^{+7}	G^+	GAUG 7	G^{7+}	$G^{7(\#5)}$	G^{7+}
G^{+9}	G^{9+}	$G^{7+(9)}$	$G^{9(\#5)}$	$G^{+7(9)}$	
G^{13}	$G^{9(13)}$	$G^{7(13)}$	$G^{9(ADD E)}$		
$G°$	GDIM	$G°^7$	$G−$		
G 6/9	$G^{6(ADD 9)}$	$G^{6(ADD A)}$	$G\frac{2}{6}$		
$G^{7(b5)}$	G^{7-5}	$G^{7(5b)}$	$G^{7(-5)}$		
GMI$^{7(b5)}$	G△^{7}	Gø^7	GMI$^{7-5}$	GMI$^{7(5b)}$	GMI$^{7(-5)}$
$G^{7(b9)}$	$G^{7(-9)}$	$G^{7(ADD Ab)}$	G^{9b}	G^{b9}	G^{9-}
GMI$^{(MA 7)}$	GMI$^{(ADD F\#)}$	GMI✄			
$G^{7(\#9)}$	$G^{7(+9)}$	$G^{(+9)}$	G^{+9}	$G^{7(b3)}$	G^{9+}
$G^{7(SUS)}$	$G^{7(SUS 4)}$	$G^{7(ADD C)}$	$G^{7(ALT 4TH)}$	$G^{7(+4)}$	
$G^{7(\#11)}$	G^{+11}	G^{11+}	$G^{11\#}$		

In examining the preceding chart, observe the following in particular:

1) The plus sign (+) is recommended only as an indication for "augmented". It should not be used as a substitute for a sharp.
2) The dash (–) is not recommended. As different arrangers use it to denote minor, diminished, or a flat, its use can only create confusion.
3) Lower case letters should not be used–a poorly written "mi" can appear to be "mj" and vice versa.
4) "MI" is the only indication for a minor chord.
5) "MA" is never used by itself–only as "MA7" or "MA9", as indication that the major seventh is included in the chord. Writing "GMI / GMA / " to indicate that the third of the chord changes, is not only incorrect but confusing–most players will automatically add the major seventh when encountering "MA". Some arrangers will write "MA" and intend that the major seventh be included. "GMI / G / " leaves no doubt as to the intent.
6) The "German" seven (7) is not used. Its ready adoption in America as a short-cut for writing "MA7", resulted from the misconception of a player who had seen the figure used in European manuscript writing. What he failed to understand was that Europeans draw the slash through the seven in order that it not be taken for the figure "1", which they draw as (1). It still denotes a dominant seventh. Much confusion has resulted since the original misconception, and serious rehearsal problems occur when music prepared in both Europe and America are used during the course of the same performance.

Be careful in the use of parenthese in writing altered functions. Don't allow an E7 with a flat ninth take on the appearance of an E7 followed by a C-flat ninth:

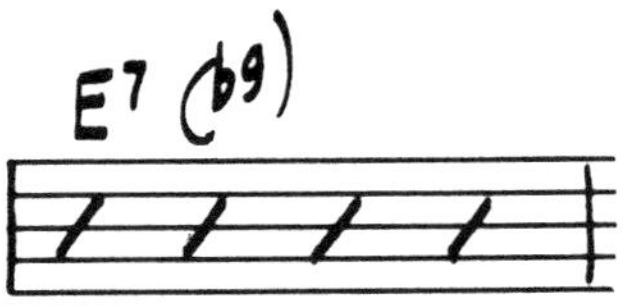

Chapter 20
PIANO PARTS

In commercial writing, many piano parts are "straight rhythm parts". The stave used for the right hand will contain slash marks, with chord symbols written above, fully written out chords, or a combination of both. The stave used for the left hand generally contains only bass notes:

Single measure repeats should not be used unless they occur in both hands in the same measure. In the next example, the abbreviations should not have been used:

Neither should two measure repeat signs be used unless they can be used on both staves. A pianist would have difficulty in sight-reading the following:

(Use of the "moustache" is optional in manuscript writing. The bar-lines connecting the two systems is adequate.)

In the preparation of other orchestral parts, measures were spaced visually. However, straight rhythm parts are best written in evenly spaced measures. The part is pre-ruled lightly in pencil, in order that space adjustments can be made if necessary to accommodate longer measures and the addition of key and time changes. The bar-lines are drawn in in ink with the aid of the straight-edge as copying progresses, or after the part is completed. Do not attempt to draw bar-lines free-hand on braced parts. (A special pre-ruled paper is available, but its use is not recommended).

As a guide in sub-dividing lines evenly, marks are placed on the leading edge of a twelve inch ruler. Sub-divisions of three, four, five and six are sufficient.

139

Straight rhythm parts are usually sufficient for instrumental arrangements. However, they are inadequate for vocal arrangements. In order to intelligently accompany a singer, the vocal line must be cued on the part. In order to keep the melody separated from the piano notes, the vocal line is usually written an octave higher than it sounds. Vocal notes are written stems–up, while piano notes are written stems–down. Slash marks are written below the stave with chord symbols directly beneath them:

Whereas the above part is complete enough for a pianist on a recording session, it would be inadequate for a night club pianist, who might also double as conductor, or work with a vocalist sans orchestra. In addition to the vocal line, the following should be cued on the part: The introduction, all interludes, modulations, and the ending. Such cues may be written where they sound, or an octave higher if necessary to maintain separation:

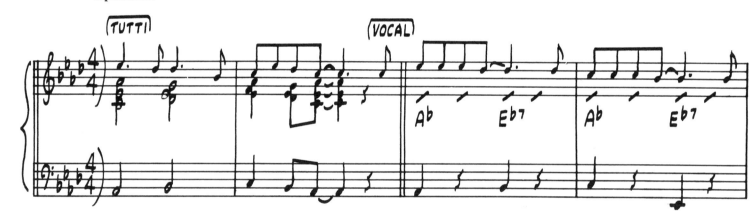

(In such a part , exceptions must be made for the direction of ties. Note that all ties in the cues are up, while those in the right hand of the piano are down):

Much time should be devoted to the study of engraved piano parts to gain familiarity with the different situations that occur in piano notation. Also review chapter nine, which dealt with the correct way of writing chords, and the placement of accidentals and ties. The two following examples contain the type of situations that should be studied in engraved music:

A proper study of engraved music will aid in being able to correctly write a passage such as the following which might be encountered in a score:

The above example written correctly:

(Note the indication used to move the left hand to the upper stave and then back again.)

The following: Is better written for the pianist as:

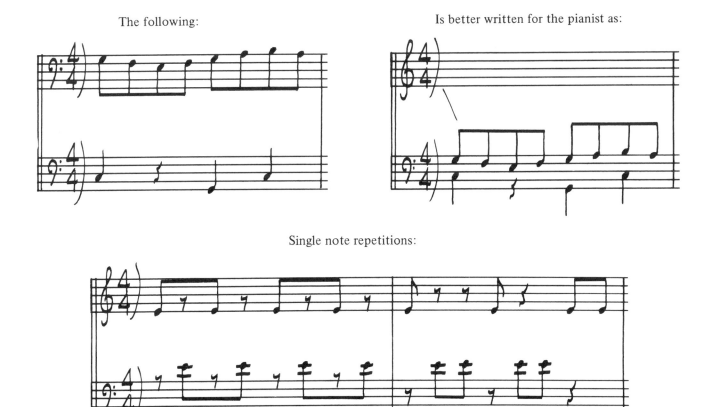

Single note repetitions:

Are correctly written as shown in the next example. It is not necessary to include the rests, as proper stemming and beaming makes the intent clear:

The preceding example notated correctly:

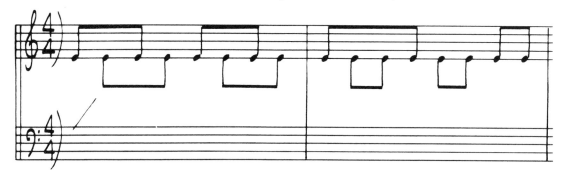

Another example of clear intent by proper stemming and beaming:

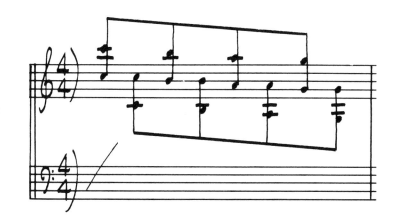

Abbreviations such as the following may be used only with caution. It is advisable that the notes be written out in full:

An "8" placed under left hand notes:

Indicates that the lower octave is to be played in addition to the written note:

Arpeggios are indicated with a wavy line placed directly before the notes:

If accidentals occur in the chord, the wavy line is placed before them:

Three incorrect placements of the arpeggio symbol:

Extended arpeggios are sometimes written out in full, but most generally they are abbreviated. The glissando symbol is used, but clarified with the addition of the indication "arp":

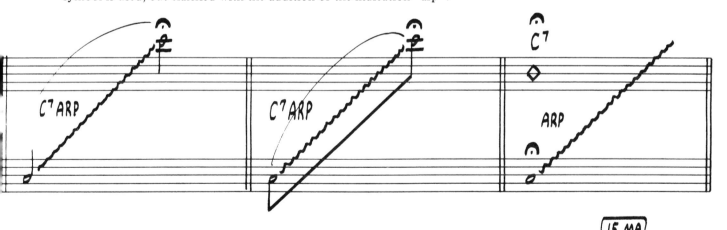

As an interval of two octaves is a fifteenth, a note to be played two octaves higher is marked:

And not as: Or as:

Seldom encountered is the indication for a note to be played three octaves higher:

Many contemporary recordings resulted from "head" arrangements worked out during the course of a recording session, during which, the musicians improvised from a "master rhythm part". The arranger wrote a basic routine along with a few suggested rhythm patterns. Such parts are copied on onion skin paper and enough copies printed for each player. If the part is not too involved, the vocal should be cued. However, it is generally omitted in order to avoid a cluttered part. Bass notes are written in the bass instrument's register—the pianist and organist will play them an octave lower than written. Such a part might appear like this:

(Once the basic rhythm track has been completed, and the vocalist added, a "sweetening" session may be held. For this, the arranger will write instrumental parts, and perhaps add a vocal group, which will be overdubbed onto the rhythm and vocal tracks.)

Chapter 21
HARP PARTS

A knowledge of the mechanics, techniques, problems and limitations of the harp is essential to the copyist. Recommended study is the section devoted to the instrument in *Orchestration* by Cecil Forsyth. If possible ask a harpist for a demonstration and further explanation of this unusual instrument.

The average harp part copied, consists mainly of chords, arpeggios, broken chords and glissandos:

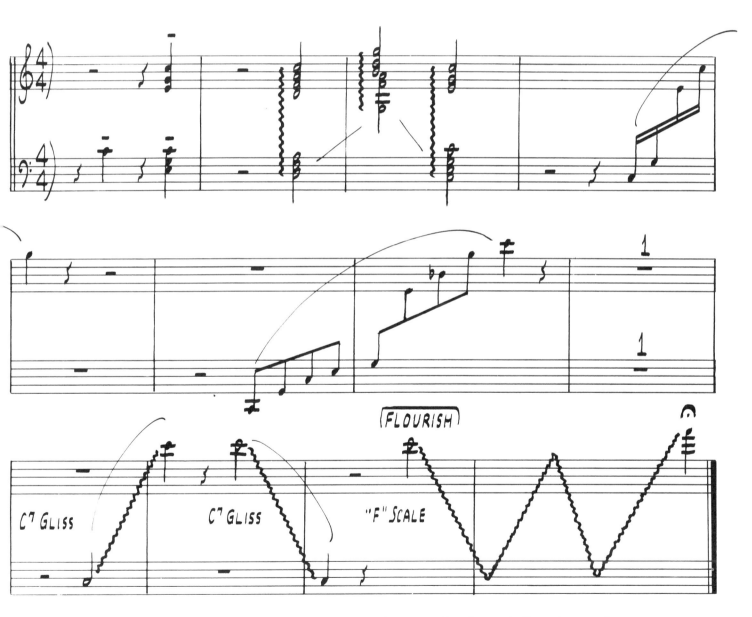

Most arrangers leave it to the harpist to mark changes on the part, rather than to indicate them on the score. Each harpist has his own preference to one of three ways of pedal notation. Regardless of the system used, all pertinent accidentals are still written on the part.

The next example shows each of the three different notations used for pedal changes:

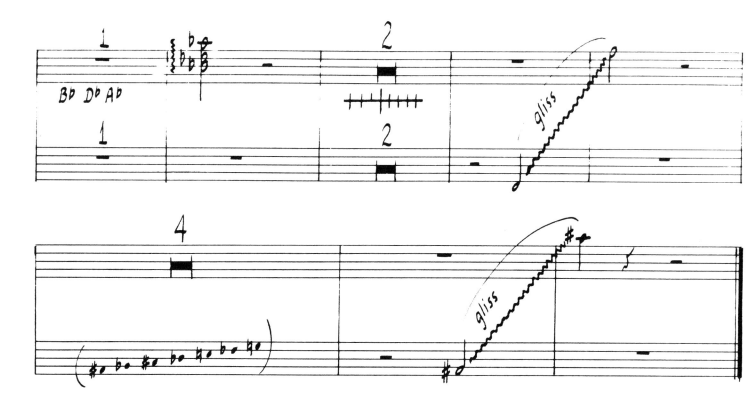

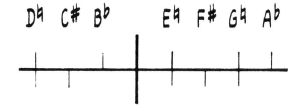

(If pedal changes are notated by the arranger, the copyist must give as much advance notice as possible when preparing the part.)

The diagram used in the third measure of the above example is used to show one of three different positions for each of the seven pedals:

When pedal changes are not indicated, glissandos are written in one of two different ways:

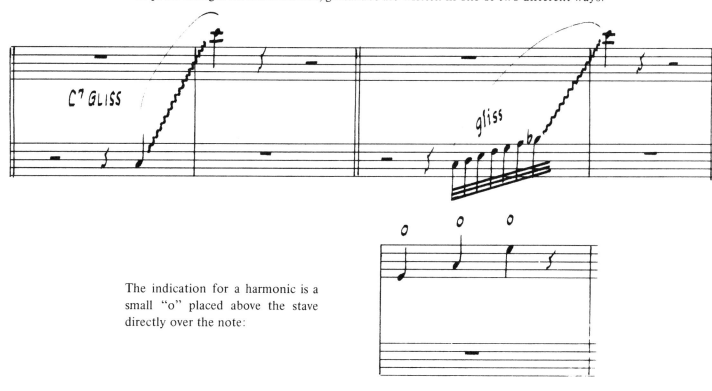

The indication for a harmonic is a small "o" placed above the stave directly over the note:

146

Chapter 22
STRING PARTS

Copying a single line string part poses no more problems than exist in the preparation of any other single line part.

In symphonic copying, separate parts are made for the "A" (1st) violins and the "B" (2nd) violins. The violas are usually combined on one part, as are the cellos.

In commercial writing, all violins are generally combined on one part. Onion skin paper is used, and as two players read from each stand, half as many parts are printed as there are players. Viola, cello and bass parts will be copied on onion skin only if there are more than two players in each section.

The average violin part consists of unisons, two and three part divisi, with occasional four part divisi. The part is generally braced, although long passages of unison and/or two part divisi may be written on a single line.

Traditionally, two part divisi occurring on the same line is written with two sets of stems:

In commercial writing, one set of stems is acceptable:

However, traditional stemming practices should be used in the following cases:

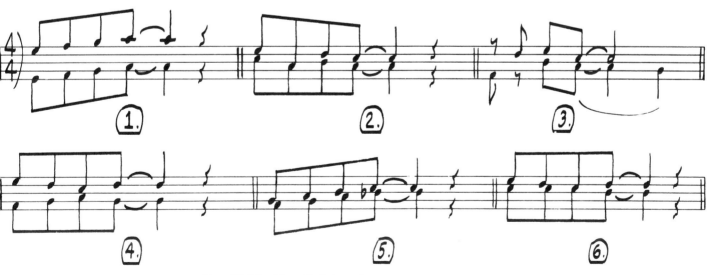

1) Divisi with wide intervals.
2) Divisi with the occasional occurrence of a unison note.
3) Divisi with the occurrence of a rest, and/or a moving voice in one part.
4) Contrapuntal parts.
5) Divisi in seconds.
6) Divisi with the occurrence of seconds and unisons.

Divisi parts are written on scores in a variety of ways:

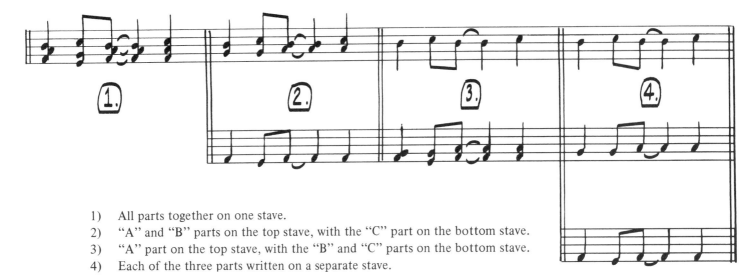

1) All parts together on one stave.
2) "A" and "B" parts on the top stave, with the "C" part on the bottom stave.
3) "A" part on the top stave, with the "B" and "C" parts on the bottom stave.
4) Each of the three parts written on a separate stave.

Regardless of how the parts are written on the score, it is best that the copyist combine them on the composite part with the "A" and "C" violins on the top stave, and the "B" violins on the bottom stave:

An added "D" violin, as a fourth harmony part, would be combined with the "B" violin on the bottom stave:

(The separation of the parts into open intervals gives the players easier to read parts.)

Arrangers will use parenthesized numbers to denote changes in the amount of players he wants on each part:

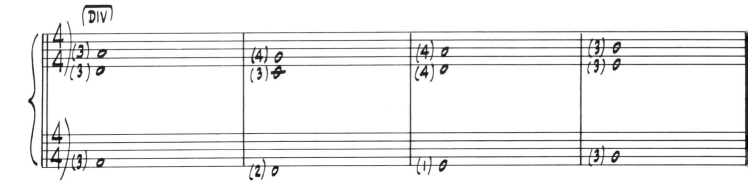

If the preceding example was copied "as is" for the violin section, confusion would result because of players jumping back and forth between lines in the attempt to maintain the requested divisions. The copyist should edit such occurrences, and strive for clarification by keeping the same number of players on each line at all times:

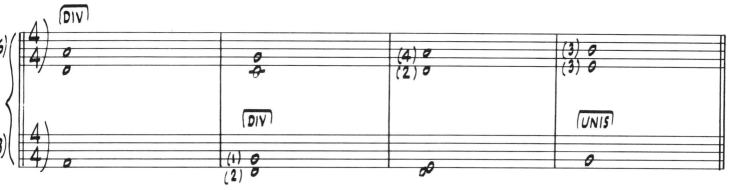

If a single line part containing changes of division, such as the following, is written on the score:

It would be better written by the copyist on a braced part, once again keeping the same number of players on each stave:

(Never write parts that force players to jump back and forth from one stave to the other.)

A short solo violin passage can sometimes be incorporated on a braced part:

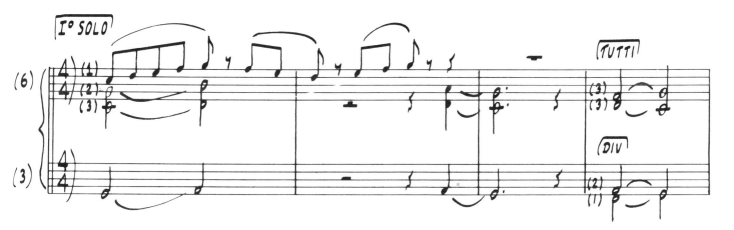

149

However, it is usually better (and in certain cases, absolutely necessary), that a three-line part be used, with the solo violin written on the added line:

(Note that in both the preceding examples that clear directions were given to the solo violinist as to when to rejoin the section.)

The "down bow" is indicated:    "Up bow" as:

These bowing symbols are always placed above the notes and above the stave. If the notes are accented, the accent symbols are placed *between* the notes and the symbols:

Double stops are indicated with a bracket to the left of the notes. If accidentals occur, the bracket is to the left of them as well. A separate bracket is written for each group of notes, except for passages such as the one in the following example. The return to divisi must be indicated:

Natural harmonics are indicated with a small "o" placed above the notes and above the stave:

In engraved music, an artificial harmonic is indicated with a small diamond written a perfect fourth above the note, and connected to the note with the stem. The diamond is always "open", regardless of the value of the note:

In manuscript writing, a triangular shaped note-head is some-times used as an alternative to the diamond:

Pizzicato is abbreviated "pizz". The indication is placed *over* the first note of the affected passage. The return to "arco" must always be shown. This indication is also placed over the first note of the affected passage:

If half the section is to play pizzicato, and the other half arco, there is no need for the part to be braced. The following indication is acceptable:

Either of the following indications is acceptable:

The following is acceptable in divisi writing:

However, this example is cluttered. A braced part should be used:

The following two variants of the same abbreviation may be safely used for pianists and guitarists, but should never be written for string players. All notes must be written out in full:

Although the following short-cut may be found on scores, such may not be used for string players. Write the missing notes in full on the part:

Analyze the composite violin part on the next page:

151

In the preceding example, note:

1) The "moustache" is always used when the part is braced.
2) The separation marking used when the part moves from a two line system to a single line and back again.
3) Each stave has its own markings and dynamics.
4) When two sets of stems become preferable to the use of one set.

(Mute indications, as well as directions for pizzicato and arco, must appear over both staves of a braced part, while ritards, accelerandos, etc., must be written under both staves. Major tempo indications are written only above the top stave and properly boxed.)

With one set of stems, accents, slurs, etc., need be stated only once:

In stems—up, stems—down writing, each part must carry its own set of markings:

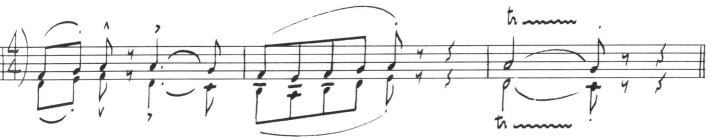

The following direction is sometimes used on violin parts:

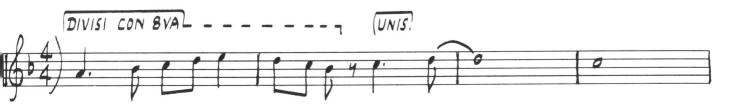

The section will automatically divide, and play it as:

Divisi tremulants may be written in either of the following ways:

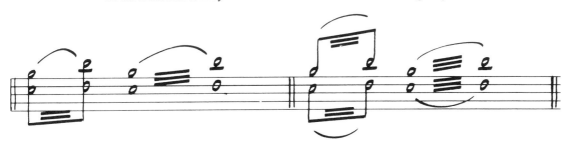

153

The following type of divisi tremulants must be written braced. The attempt to write them on a single line can only result in confusion:

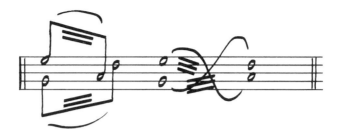

Viola and cello parts generally consist of unison with only occasional two part divisi. Hence, these parts are copied in much the same manner as single line orchestral parts. Black and white parts are prepared when there are only one or two players per section. Onion skin paper will be used when there are three or more players in the individual section.

Three and four part divisi is sometimes encountered:

Simple passages, such as the first of the above examples, can safely be written on one line. However, four part divisi, and more complex passages, should be written braced:

With the occurrence of consistent three and four part divisi in large viola and/or cello sections, it would be best to prepare separate composite parts.

Bass players also read two to the stand. The parts are largely unison or octaves, so they may safely be written on a single line. The direction, "½ Pizz, ½ Arco", frequently occurs.

Always be on the alert for page turns on braced parts. Remember that half the section is forced to drop out to turn pages if a "V.S." has not been used.

Chapter 23
VOCAL PARTS, LEAD SHEETS AND SONG COPIES

Proportional spacing of notes cannot apply to vocal writing. Spacing is determined by the length of words and syllables. Due to the extra space required, it is seldom that vocal parts can be written four measures to the line. Most generally, they are written in combinations of three and four measures per line, with an occasional occurence of two measures on a line.

A straight-edge is used as a guide in printing lyrics. Words and syllables are centered as nearly as possible directly under the accompanying notes:

A AN AND SAND SHAND PHLAND A PHLINX PINKS PI AND RHO TAUME

(In traditional writing, each note carries its own flag—beams are infrequently used. This practice is now considered obsolescent, and beams are in general use in vocal writing. However, four eighth notes are seldom beamed together—it is best that each beat be separate and complete in itself.)

Hyphens are used to separate syllables, and "extender" lines used for sustained words and/or final syllables:

AL-WAYS THOUGHT THAT SOME-DAY WE'D BE _____

Syllable hyphens are extended when they occur under ties and/or sustained notes:

FOR   EV - - - - - - - ER AND   AL - - - - - - - WAYS _____

Parts are extremely difficult to read if hyphens and extender lines are not used:

ALWAYS THOUGHT THAT SOMEDAY WE'D BE

Bad practices can result from not allowing sufficient space under the notes for the lyrics:

AL-WAYS THOUGHT THAT SOME-DAY
WE'D BE _____

An improper alignment of lyrics beneath notes is inexcusable:

AL-WAYS THOUGHT THAT SOME-DAY WE'D BE _____

A small "x" is used in place of note-heads for spoken passages. The proper direction is also indicated on the part:

AN-Y-WHERE YOU GO I'LL BE THERE, JUST BE SURE THAT IN YOUR HEART ___

Vocal parts, such as used on recording sessions, are titled and layed out as in the following example:

MICKIE

Arranged By
LARRY CANSLER

MICKIE FINN

ENCHANTED ISLE

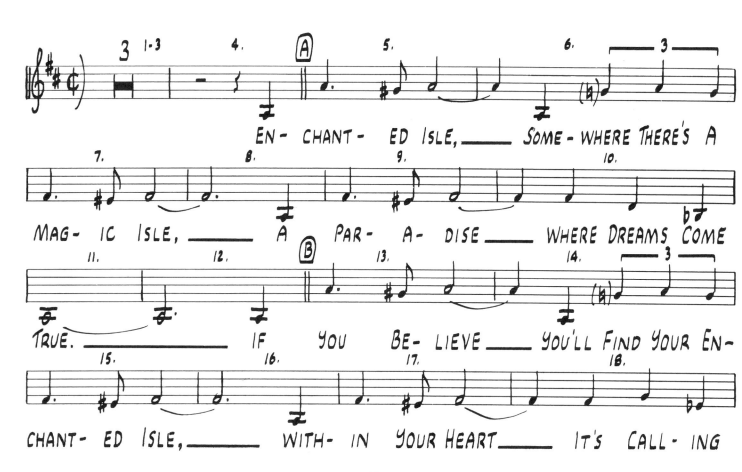

EN - CHANT - ED ISLE, _____ SOME - WHERE THERE'S A

MAG - IC ISLE, _____ A PAR - A- DISE _____ WHERE DREAMS COME

TRUE. _____ IF YOU BE- LIEVE _____ YOU'LL FIND YOUR EN-

CHANT- ED ISLE, _____ WITH- IN YOUR HEART _____ IT'S CALL-ING

(Note in the preceding example that an exception has been made to the location of bar numbers.)

"Lead sheets" are prepared by the copyist in order that composers have copies of their songs for submission to artists, recording companies and publishers, as well as for the purpose of copyright. Lead sheets are copied on onion skin paper, and sufficient copies printed for the composer's requirements. Lead sheets are prepared in the same manner as vocal parts, but with the addition of chord symbols placed above the notes. Such a part would be titled and written as follows:

The pertinent copyright information is printed at the bottom of the first page:

© 1960 MORELLA MUSIC CO., NORTH HOLLYWOOD, CALIF. 91607

The composer who desires to submit something more complete than a lead sheet, will prepare a "song copy." As these are three line parts, the copyist will use 12-line onion skin paper. On the following page is an example of the way a song copy is titled and copied. Again, the pertinent copyright information is printed at the bottom of the first page:

LOVE CAN NEVER, EVER BE
A ONE WAY STREET

By { VAN ALEXANDER - A.S.C.A.P.
     STEVE GRAHAM - A.S.C.A.P.

In the preceding example, the title and credit were written in the space of one stave. This was made possible because of the four bar introduction. Ordinarily, the title will occupy the space of three staves. If special paper is not available, blank onion skin paper may be pieced in and attached with *Scotch Transparent Tape.*

Shown below is a title which occupies the space of three staves. Credits are always written below the title— Lyric credits to the left, while music credits are to the right:

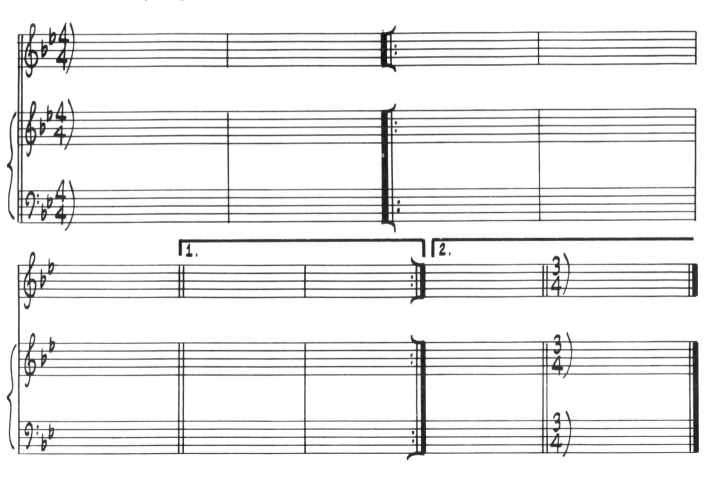

I Could Write A Book

WORDS BY
LORENZ HART

MUSIC BY
RICHARD RODGERS

Use the following example as a layout guide in the preparation of song copies containing repeat signs, and time and/or key changes:

(Clef and key signatures are always carried in song copies, and the "moustache" is always used.)

If a choir is used on an arrangement, the singer must have notification of singing solo or if the part is to be phrased with the choir:

AN-Y-WHERE YOU GO I'LL BE THERE, JUST BE SURE THAT IN YOUR HEART___

Single measure and two measure repeats may never be used on a vocal part, nor may the part contain first and second endings or a dal segno. The part must be written out in full continuity.

Although first and second endings may not be used on solo vocal parts, they are acceptable in lead sheets and song copies. Adjustments, such as for the addition of small notes, dashed ties, stems—down, etc., must be made if the second set of lyrics does not match the first set:

1. I ON-LY___ MEANT TO LOVE YOU DID-N'T YOU
2. KILL A MAN WITH A BOT-TLE OF POI-SON OR A

(Excerpt is from "The Chokin' Kind", used by permission of Wilderness Music Publishing Co., Inc.)

Slurred syllables are accompanied with slurs and extender lines:

FIRE,___ THEN ALL___ WHO WERE

It is advisable to keep a dictionary available to aid in the proper hyphenation of words, i.e., fall-ing, run-ning, o-ver, ev-er, ev-'ry, ver-y, etc.

Chapter 24
CHOIR PARTS

The traditional method of writing choir parts include the use of separate stems and flags for each note. Also, an "8" is attached to the treble clef of the tenor part, indicating that the notes sound an octave lower than written:

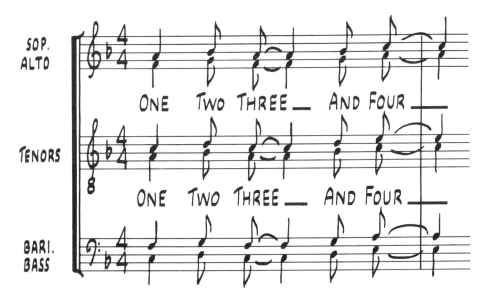

(As choir parts are generally three or four system parts, it is necessary that they be copied on 12-line onion skin paper. One part is printed for each two singers. Observe that lyrics need be written only twice on a three system part.)

Today's singers are perfectly capable of reading beamed notes, and actually prefer such notation rather than the traditional. The clef with the added "8" is not necessary for the tenors–the actual sound of the notes is taken for granted. The use of the bracket on the part is optional:

(As in the case of any braced part, all notes must have correct vertical alignment.)

161

Three voices can often be safely accomodated on one line:

Division, and changes therein, must be indicated for singers, as they are for string players:

Four system parts require only three sets of lyrics:

In duet writing, the occurence of intervals of the second require the use of two sets of stems. Continue using two sets until the occurence of a rest allows the return to one set:

Traditionally, two sets of stems are used on the same line for unison passages:

Two sets of stems are not necessary
in manuscript writing if the part is
correctly marked. The omission of
all superfluous material contributes
to a less cluttered part:

If a part is properly marked, two sets of stems are not necessary for parts moving from harmony to unison
and back to harmony:

In the following instance, two sets of stems would be necessary to clarify the passage:

Although wide intervals may be
written with one set of stems, it is
generally advisable to use two sets:

Two sets of stems are always used when crossed voices occur within a passage. It is not only essential that
proper stem direction be maintained in such a case, but also that arrows be used for added clarification.
The use of two sets should be continued until such time as a rest permits the return to one set of stems:

Although four eighth notes are ordinarily beamed together:

It is advisable to write in groups of individual beats for all singers:

Analyze the example of choir writing appearing on the next page:

163

Choirs (vocal groups) are frequently used as another section of the orchestra, and sing little more than syllables. Such a part might look like the following:

(Observe that complete dynamic markings must accompany each line of a choir part.)

165

Chapter 25

CONDUCTOR PARTS

In commercial writing, a conductor part is a very highly condensed and compressed version of the score. Although moving voices are sometimes indicated, it is seldom that any actual harmony will be shown.

Conductor parts are always made for arrangements that will be used in night clubs, concerts, etc. The conductor cannot be expected to fight with a stack of scores, devoting more time to turning pages than in conducting the orchestra.

On recording sessions, conductors generally prefer to work from scores. However, even in this case, a conductor part is prepared for the use of the producer and/or engineer of the session. The part is titled as either "Production" or "Booth Part". In the event the conductor prefers to make the first run through from the score, then switch to a conductor part for the "takes", it becomes necessary that the part be copied on onion skin paper, and parts printed for both the conductor and the producer.

In motion picture and film television recording, an extra part is printed for the music cutter. It is used during the course of the session to check timings, and then again in the final work of laying the music track onto the film.

In order that conductor parts may be fully utilized, they must be made as complete as possible in the limited amount of space that exists. All information contained on the score must be shown—vocal melody plus lyrics, each instrumental line with its proper identification, tempo markings, dynamics, accents, and anything else that is pertinent.

The example shown on the following three pages is the actual Conductor/Booth Part used for a recording by *The Golddiggers* on Metromedia Record # MD 1009. In analyzing the part, note the following:

1) Note-heads must be made somewhat smaller than normal.
2) Length of stems are usually shorter than normal.
3) Lyrics are written above the notes to avoid clutter.
4) Measures are evenly spaced if possible.
5) Proportional spacing cannot always exist in the orchestra line because of considerations that must be made in the vocal line.
6) The orchestra line is generally written as a divisi part. Whole note rests are carried after one section drops out.
7) Tempo indications are written above the vocal line if possible. (In this example, it was necessary to place the "rubato" in bar # 49 below the vocal line in order to avoid clutter with the low ledger lines and markings in bar # 44. Observe that the "rubato" was enclosed in a complete box in this instance, rather than in a three-sided box that would have been used had it been possible to write the direction above the vocal line.)
8) The "ritard" in bar # 48 was placed between the two staves and underlined. Any similiar directions would have been written in the same manner.
9) Bar numbers are written between the two staves and centered within the measure when possible.
10) Three different musical lines must occasionally be written on the one orchestral line.
11) Key changes (and/or time changes) occurring at the beginning of a line are pre-stated at the end of the preceding line.
12) All entrances are indicated and boxed. Observe the difference in the box when it is used below the stave.
13) That the orchestra line is consistently in treble clef, and that an "8 VA BASSO" marking became necessary in bar # 44 to avoid clutter.
14) Five measures per line were used in the last two braces in order to keep the part from going two measures onto a fourth page.

Arranged By
VAN ALEXANDER

BLAME IT ON MY YOUTH

("Blame It On My Youth" used with the permission of T.B. Harms Company.)

Conductor parts for simple instrumental arrangements can most often be written on a single line:

For more complex arrangements, it is better to use a braced part utilizing both treble and bass clefs. In this type of part, it becomes possible to write all instruments where they sound:

(Occasionally a vocal arrangement will require a three system part, either because of a duet that cannot be written on the one vocal line, or because of an overly complicated orchestral part which requires two lines. Also, instrumental conductor parts for symphonic size orchestras will demand that a three, or even four, system part be written. In all these cases, 12-stave paper should be used.)

Simple orchestral passages may be written without resorting to stems—up, stems—down writing:

Always look ahead at the score and be prepared for what is coming next. Avoid writing a single line part that should have been written divisi:

Proper planning can only result by looking ahead at the score:

170

Ad lib fills and breaks may be indicated as in the following example:

Although instruments should be written where they sound, clutter can sometimes result:

In the above example, the saxes would be better written an octave lower than they sound, and so stated, with the return to "loco" marked at a logical place:

A reminder to "carry" whole measure rests:

The preceding example is far preferable to the following:

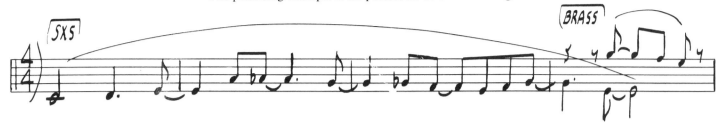

The following is a condensed version of a rubato passage as it might be written on a score:

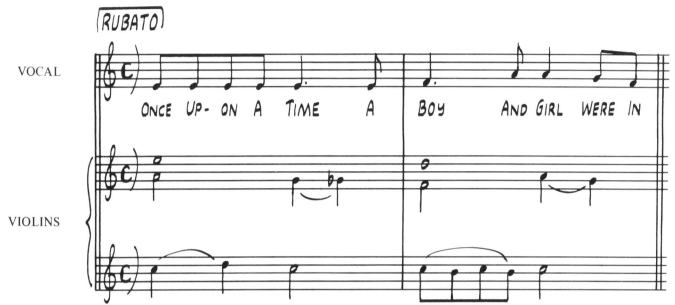

Giving the conductor the vocal and only the lead voice of the instrumental line is insufficient for his needs in a section that is out of tempo:

In any such rubato passage, the conductor must be made aware of all moving voices:

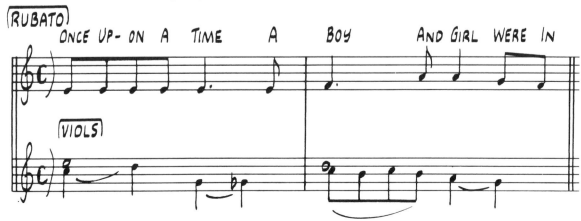

"Breaks" and the resumption of rhythm must be shown on conductor parts:

The addition of a choir (vocal group) will turn the vocal line into a divisi part. The lead line of the choir must generally be written an octave lower than it sounds in order to maintain separation:

Indication must be noted when the soloist and choir are singing together or separately:

If the orchestra is tacet for more than a few measures, it should be indicated as follows:

Changes of rhythmic patterns should be indicated:

173

A simple third orchestral line consisting largely of half or whole notes may be indicated as in the following example ("SXS SUSTAIN UNDER"), thereby avoiding an overly complicated single line orchestral part, or the necessity of taking the orchestra to a brace:

Long ad lib solos, and/or extended ad lib fills, may be indicated on the conductor part as in the following example. The end of such solos or fills must also be indicated:

For night club acts, a dual purpose "piano-conductor" part is sometimes made in place of separate cued piano parts and conductor parts. Such parts are made in much the same manner as song copies. 12-stave onion skin paper is used and two copies are printed.

Such piano-conductor parts are made in one of two ways:

1) The orchestra is written on the first of the three staves, with the vocal written on the upper stave of the piano part. By necessity, the vocal line must generally be written an octave higher than it sounds:

2) The vocal is written on the first of the three staves, generally where it sounds, and lyrics written above the notes. As many orchestral cues as possible will be written on the top stave of the piano part—the actual sound of the instruments can seldom be considered, as the notes must be kept separated from those of the piano:

(The first of the two methods is not desirable, for it is all but impossible to include the lyrics, which are a necessity, especially during rubato passages.)

(Regardless of how well piano-conductor parts are made, they tend to become extremely cluttered. The pianist is given more information than he requires, while the conductor receives an insufficiency. A fully cued piano part is generally more than adequate for a night club pianist, even though he "doubles" as conductor, and a complete conductor part is more ideal for the conductor than is a piano-conductor part. Nonetheless, these parts are frequently called for, and the copyist must be prepared to make them. Planning, layout and actual writing require considerable time, so it is advisable to spend time in the practice of making these parts.)

Only easily understood abbreviations should be used in conductor parts. In the following list, recommended abbreviations (or the use of none) are listed in the second column, while the third column consists of those that should be avoided:

Woodwinds	WW's	Woods, Winds, Reeds
Alto Saxophone(s)	Alto(s)	Al(s)., Al. Sx(s).
Tenor Saxophone	Tenor	Tn., Tnr.
Baritone Saxophone	Bari.	B.S., Bry., Bary.
Bass Saxophone	Bass Sx.	B.S., Bs. Sx.
Saxophones	Sxs.	Saxes
Soprano Saxophone	Sop. Sx.	Sp. Sx.
Clarinet(s)	Clar(s).	Cl(s)., Clt(s).
Flute(s)	(None)	Fl(s)., Flt(s).
Alto Flute	(None)	Al. Fl., Alt. Flt.
Bass Clarinet	Bass Clar.	B. Cl., Bs. Cl., Bs. Clt.
Contra Bass Clarinet	C. B. Clar.	CB. CL.
Bassoon(s)	Bsn(s).	Bs., Bn.
Horn(s)	(None)	Hn(s), Fr. Hn(s)., F. Hn(s).
Trumpet(s)	Trpt(s).	Tp(s)., Tr(s)., Trp(s)., Trt(s).
Trombone(s)	Trom(s).	Tb(s)., Tr(s)., Trb(s)., Bone(s)
Flugelhorn	Flugel.	F. Hn., Fl. Hn.
Bass Trombone	Bass Trom.	Bs. Tb., B. Tb., Bs. Bone
Tuba	(None)	Tb., Tba., Tu.
Violin(s)	Viol(s)	Vl(s)., Vio(s)., Vi(s).

Viola(s)	(None)	Vl(s)., Va(s)., Vla(s).
Cello(s) (Celli)	(None)	Cl., Clo., V.C., Cel.
Bass	(None)	Bs., Ba., C. B.
Fender Bass	(None)	F. B., F.Bs.
Drums	(None)	Dr., Drs.
Percussion	Perc.	Pc., Pn.
Tympani	Tymp.	Tym., Tim.
Timbales	(None)	Tim., Timb.
Tambourine	Tamb.	Tam.
Tam Tam	(None)	Tam., T. T.
Tom Tom(s)	Tom(s)	T. T. (s)
Triangle	Tria.	Tr., Tri.
Bells	(None)	Bl., Bls.
Glockenspiel	Glock.	Gl., Glk.
Piano	(None)	Pno., Pia., Pi., Pn.
Celeste	(None)	Cl., Cel., Cste.
Harp	(None)	Hp., Hrp.
Xylophone	Xylo	Xyl.
Vibraphone	Vibes	Vib., Vibs.
Strings	Stgs.	Sts.
Guitar	Guit.	Gt., Gtr.
Bass Guitar	Bass. Guit.	B. G., Bs. Gt.
Electric Guitar	Elec. Guit.	E. G., El. Gt.
12 String Guitar	12 Stg. Guit.	12 S. G., 12 St. Gt.
Vocal	Voc. or None	Vo., Vc., Vcl.
Vocal Group (Choir)	Group, Choir	Vcl. Gp., Grp., Cho.
Cup Mute Brass	Cup Brass	Cup Br.
Harmon Mute Brass	Harm. Brass	Hr. Br.
Straight Mute Brass	St. M. Brass	S. M. Br.
Plunger Mute Brass	Plgr. Brass	Pl. Br.
Open Brass	(None)	Op. Br.
Brass In Stands	(None)	Br. In St.
8 VA	(None)	8
8 VA Bassa	(None)	8 VB, 8B

As a general rule, it is best to construct the conductor part before beginning to copy the individual orchestra parts, as more discrepancies and mistakes in the score can be located when an overall view is taken. In addition, an advance familiarity with the score is gained, which will be beneficial in planning the layout of individual parts.

Chapter 26
COPYING FROM SKETCH

At times it becomes necessary for the copyist to prepare orchestral parts directly from an abbreviated score (sketch). This occurs most often in the field of motion pictures and filmed television, where sometimes time does not permit having an orchestrator prepare a full score.

Presented below is an example of what such a sketch might look like. The instrumentation is for 5 saxophones (2 altos, 2 tenors, 1 baritone), 5 trumpets, 4 trombones, drums, guitar, bass and piano. The drum part is not written on the sketch, and it is necessary to construct it from the other rhythm parts:

In working directly from sketch, one must always remember what has been copied before, in order that mistakes are not made in doublings and omissions.

Although one may never be called upon to copy from sketch, the copyist should have the ability, understanding and knowledge to cope with the situation should it arise. It may someday become necessary to extract parts for an orchestra as large as symphony size written in little more space than the example quoted above.

PRACTICE: Extract the various parts from the sketch and compare results with those given on the next two pages:

TRUMPETS

TROMBONES

178

SAXOPHONES

RHYTHM

Chapter 27
COPYING FOR PUBLISHERS

So called "educational music" is usually prepared by copyists rather than engravers.

An unfortunate tradition existing among publishers of such music, dictates that no blank staves or measures be at the end of individual parts—the final double bar must be located at the end of the last stave. The thinking involved, is that the purchaser might feel cheated if the pages are not completely full. As a result, parts are either "spread" or "crowded", for the copyist can give little consideration to properly balanced and phrased parts.

The length of each part must be pre-computed before it is copied. This is best accomplished by making a chart for each instrument, or section, providing all instruments within the section are the same. From the chart, it can be determined if 7, 8, 9, 10 or 12 line paper be used, or combinations of these. The chart is then used as a guide in copying the part. It aids in the determination of how much space to allow for multiple bar rests, and which measures should be spread or crowded in order to make the part come out even at the end of the last stave.

In preparing the chart:
  1) Assume that two pages of 10-line paper will be sufficient.
  2) Assume that four measures per line will be written, allowing the space of one measure for a multiple bar rest.
  3) Go through the score, and mark an "x" on the chart for each measure which includes notes, and a figure for each multiple bar rest.
  4) Draw two parallel vertical lines on the chart to indicate the location of double bars.
  5) Allow two lines for the title.

A chart prepared in such a manner, will look like the following:

The copying of this particular part would present no problems, for the spreading of only a few measures and/or multiple bar rests would make up the deficit. The part could also be copied on two sheets of 9-line paper, and writing two lines of five measures each to compensate for the two measure overage on the nineteenth line.

Such parts are not always so simple.

As printed type will be used for instrument identifications and titles, it is sufficient for the copyist to pencil these in lightly in the space for the title. Printed type will also be used for the necessary copyright information, so this is of no concern to the copyist.

Two page parts are printed "double fold"—page 1 on the left, and page 2 to the right.

Both sides of the paper are printed on for three and four page parts. Page 2 appears on the reverse side of page 1, while page 4 appears on the reverse side of page 3. This makes it essential that page turns be planned to occur on pages 1 and 3. This can generally be achieved only by spreading or crowding the part in order to reach a multiple bar rest, for again, no blank measures or lines are permissable.

The average drum part can usually be written on one page.

The piano part can usually be contained on four pages of 12-line paper, but will likely have to be written five and six measures per line. It is doubtful if any page turns will exist.

A single line conductor part is made for instrumental arrangements, while a two line part is made for vocal arrangements—lyrics must be included. A separate vocal part will also be prepared.

Dal Segnos and Da Capos may be used only when no page turning is required to get back to the sign, or to the coda. A blank stave is not left between the main body of the arrangement and the coda. White ink of the *liquid paper* variety is used to paint out the blank portion of the staves in the indentations:

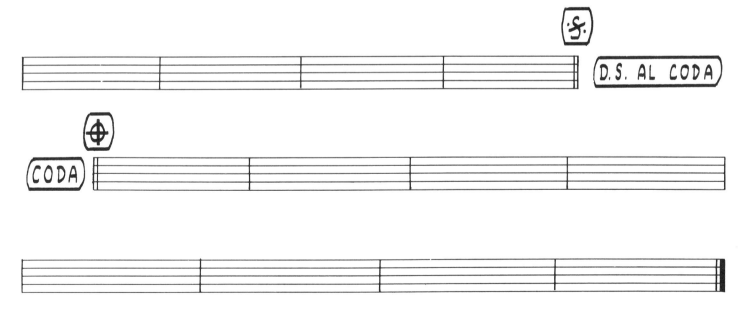

SYMPHONIC COPYING

This book has been concerned with writing an average of four measures to each stave on 10-line paper. Symphonic copying is done on paper of up to 24-lines, with as many measures to each stave as can be accomodated, and is therefore a different consideration.

One who is called upon to do this type of work, will in all probability be under the direction of a supervising copyist who will explain the specialized demands. A copyist who knows how to notate properly, and edit and space, will have no difficulty in adapting to the different demands of the symphonic field.

181

Chapter 28
CLOSING

(A PERSONAL NOTE)

This book has attempted to impart the knowledge necessary for you to become a competent music copyist, and to present as well the types of problems likely to be encountered, along with their solutions. It is hoped the information given here, enhanced by your own knowledge of music, will make of you a much better copyist and craftsman. This treatise was designed to enable you to shorten the slow process of learning the art solely by travelling the rocky road of acquired knowledge, as most were forced to do in the past. It is now your responsibility to gain experience by the act of doing.

As this experience is being acquired, consider the following:

Be your own worst critic—would you like to play from parts you have written?

Be conscientious—do *more* than the job calls for, not less.

Assume the responsibility of correcting errors in the score. A player cannot be expected to guess at what was intended—he doesn't have a copy of the score as you did.

Concentrate on the project at hand. Never allow the mind to wander when working—the part being copied at the time will also tend to wander. Copying is not a mechanical job—it is an art.

Attend as many rehearsals as possible. Observe the problems that may arise from music prepared by others, as well as your own. Learn to prevent the time-consuming questions that can bog down a rehearsal.

"Spell" and notate correctly.

Be skeptical—never take the score for granted.

There is always something new to learn. Never stop studying. Constantly expand your knowledge. If a particular problem cannot be solved, don't guess at the solution—check with the arranger before the music goes on the stands.

In summation, always:

Edit
Interpret
Space and Phrase
Maintain Balance
Simplify
Strive for Conformity
Consistency
Accuracy
Use Common Sense
Knowledge
and Logic

Good luck and good copying,

Clinton Roemer

182

ABOUT THE AUTHOR

The name of Clinton Roemer has been one of the most prominent among music copyists in Hollywood for nearly thirty years. He has worked in all fields of the entertainment industry—motion pictures, live and filmed television, phonograph recordings, dance bands, radio, symphonies, musical shows, night club acts and publishing.

For twenty-five years he was chief copyist for the Stan Kenton Orchestra, during which time music was also copied for the avant-garde Innovations and Los Angeles Neophonic Orchestras. Mr. Roemer's name is also well-known in educational circles as a result of the availability of the Kenton library to school stage bands.

While operating his own music copying service, Mr. Roemer and his staff worked with many composer/arrangers, including, Van Alexander, Warren Barker, Carl Brandt, Lou Busch, Benny Carter, Jack Fascinato, Sid Feller, Oliver Nelson, Andre Previn, Pete Rugolo and Gerald Wilson. Librarian and exclusive copyist for such artists as Peggy Lee, Gordon MacRae, George Shearing, Allan Sherman, Margaret Whiting and Nancy Wilson. Additional services were performed on a free-lance basis for many other artists and arrangers.

Prior to his retirement from active copying, he spent four years as supervising copyist of the Dean Martin television show and for Hanna-Barbera Studios, in addition to servicing his other accounts.

On a limited basis, Mr. Roemer is currently accepting clinic appearances at those educational institutions offering credit courses in music copying.